Julianna Altmann—Piroska Biczó—Gergely Buzás—István Horváth—
Annamária Kovács—Gyula Siklósi—András Végh

MEDIUM REGNI

Esztergom — István Horváth

Székesfehérvár — Gyula Siklósi

The Royal Basilica in Székesfehérvár — Piroska Biczó

Óbuda — Julianna Altmann

Visegrád — Gergely Buzás

Buda — András Végh

Customs in the Medieval Royal Court — Annamária Kovács

Julianna Altmann—Piroska Biczó—Gergely Buzás—István Horváth—
Annamária Kovács—Gyula Siklósi—András Végh

MEDIUM REGNI

Medieval
Hungarian
Royal Seats

NAP KIADÓ

NAP KIADÓ gratefully acknowledges the support
of the Ministry of National Cultural Heritage
and the Táncsics Mihály Foundation
of the Hungarian Credit Bank, MHB.

Translated by Erika Zoltán

Maps on pp 10, 44, 99, 116, 164 — details, 16th century, by Lázár
Plan on 66 — 1738

Esztergom:
Ground plans and reconstruction drawings by István Horváth, Konstantin Vukov;
photos by István Horváth, Attila Mudrák;

Székesfehérvár:
Ground plans and reconstruction drawings by Mrs Dévai, Endre Egyed;
photos by Tibor Kádas, Krisztina Pálfay;

Royal Basilica:
Drawings by Zoltán Szabó;
photos by Ferenc Gelencsér, Tibor Kádas;

Visegrád:
Drawings by Gergely Buzás, Balázs Holl, Ernő Szakál;
photos by Róbert Hack, Jenő Sebestyén;

Buda and Óbuda:
Drawings by Gergely Buzás, Zsuzsanna Kuczogi, Andrea Láng, György Szekér, András Végh;
photos by Margit Bakos, Tibor Szentpéteri, Bence Tihanyi.

Photographs have been reproduced by courtesy of the following:
Budapest Historical Museum, Hungarian National Museum, the Székesfehérvár Szent
István király Museum, as well as the illustrators and photographers.

PREFACE

FROM THE 'MIDDLE OF THE COUNTRY' TO THE CAPITAL

Professor Kumorovitz, the outstanding scholar, who died a few years ago, wrote in his study published in 1971 that in the Middle Ages the Esztergom — Székesfehérvár — Buda triangle was regarded as the 'middle of the country' (medium regni) first of all because it was easily accessible from every part of the country. Another reason was that the area to the west of the River Danube, where it flows in the north—south direction, seemed to have been more densely populated. Out of the ten bishoprics established by St. Stephen four were to be found to the west of the Danube; two, Kalocsa and Vác were near the Danube and four served the believers in the eastern parts of the country. The bishoprics in Zagreb and Nitra, founded by St. Ladislaus and King Coloman, were also in the west.

From the 11th century three settlements performed the central duties, and there were several royal mansions and hunting—seats in the 'middle of the country'. As for example in Dömös, where King Béla I had a fatal accident, and where his grandson, Prince Álmos resided later. It has to be known that in the first centuries of the Middle Ages the sovereigns had no seats, thus — at least in the present meaning — no capital either. The kings and princes regularly travelled through their country, and they either stayed in one of their mansions or palaces (cf. the German 'Pfalz') scattered around the country or were invited by prelates and ecclesiastical boards. The specialist literature calls this 'travelling government' (Reiseherrschaft). This was completely suitable for the royal household: they consumed the tax in kind, attended to the businesses of their subjects not willing to go on long and tiring journeys. The government of the country was where the sovereign was staying. It was already a more developed phase when the king always kept a certain celebration at the same place (church). Thus the subjects could predict when and where they were able to see the sovereign.

The situation was the same in the age of the Árpáds, but there already existed more or less permanent centres. The most important was Esztergom. The king visited the castle built here the most frequently until the 13th century. St. Stephen founded the first archdiocese of the country here, thus Esztergom became the ecclesiastical centre of the country, and it still is. The part of the king's income which he did not consume during his travelling in the country was sent and collected here at least in the age of King Coloman, or it had to be accounted for.

The second centre was Székesfehérvár. The kings were crowned, St. Stephen and St. Emeric were buried there. Székesfehérvár remained the most often used royal burial—place in later times as well. As extremely many pilgrims gathered here for St. Stephen's day, the king had assizes every year as it was ordained in paragraph 1 of the Golden Bull (1222). The role of the third centre was the least known for quite a long time. This centre, Buda (the present Óbuda) was also one of the settlements in the 'middle of the country'. The king spent the Lent here in his mansion, later (from the beginning of the 13th century) in his castle.

The middle of the 13th century and the foundation of the new Buda did not bring any change in the role of the 'medium regni'. Buda gradually became first, the most significant town, then the capital of the country because of its economic importance and the royal residence there though for the time being it was not permanent. At the beginning of the 14th century it is mentioned as the 'seat, the centre of the country and the biggest town'. So King Charles Robert was laid out here before the burial in Székesfehérvár; and the new king, Luis the Great came here first to receive the deference of his burghers. It was the right and the duty of the Buda burghers to guard the doors of the royal cathedral under arms during the coronation of the new king.

So from the beginning of the 14th century Buda was considered to be the capital of the country in spite of the fact that no sovereign resided here in the bigger part of the century. The king mostly stayed in Visegrád, which also belonged to the 'middle of the country', and which can already be called residence. In the late Middle Ages the capital and the royal residence in Hungary, just like in many other countries in Europe were not necessarily at the same place. The role of the capital was constitutional as well as economic. The residence was the place and building complex where one part of the king's household (and the connected royal offices and courts) stayed when the sovereign and the acccompanying household (either to arrange public affairs or for enjoyment) were away. Such residences appeared mainly in the late Middle Ages; they were not needed in the time of the earlier 'travelling governments'. So it was of special importance that Charles Robert entrusted the ecclesiastical body of the royal chapel with notorial functions. In the 1370s it ceased to function, but then the bailiff of the royal chapel received the royal medium seal and thus he took the lead of the 'audience': he designated the competent judges for the suits. Such and similar administrative and judical procedures needed a place where clients were audited when the sovereign and most of his household were away.

At the beginning of the 15th century the royal household moved to Buda, which thus became not only the capital but also the royal residence. Though the royal chapel did not have the notorial functions any more from the end of Sigismund's reign, the royal court of justice worked regularly. The Treasury reorganized by King Matthias was in charge of the receipts and expenditures of the country in the absence of the sovereign as well. When the Treasurer accompanied the King, his deputy remained in Buda with one part of the office. From the second third of the 15th century the Parliament was meeting more and more often and later regularly in Buda or Pest. When all the nobility had to be present, the Parliament met in

Rákos mező, near Pest. In the 14th century most prelates and noblemen bought houses first in Visegrád then in Buda, because if they wanted to fulfil their functions as royal councillors, they had to live in the vicinity of the royal residence.

So by the end of the Middle Ages Buda (partly with its sister towns) became the centre of the 'middle of the country'. However, this did not mean that the duties connected with the centre of the country were not shared between the settlements of the region. Székesfehérvár remained not only the coronation town but also the burial—place of most kings. The ecclesiastical centre of the country continued to be Esztergom; and as Cardinal Dénes Szécsi managed to confirm the rights of the Esztergom Cardinal as primate and 'born papal legate', he became the head of the Hungarian church, who — by right of 'the papal legate' was entitled to administer justice in suits of the Holy See, even if appeals were lodged from the dioceses belonging to the Bishop of Kalocsa. Thus Esztergom was the centre of the ecclesiastical judical centre as well. (In the Middle Ages many more cases belonged to the ecclesiastical courts than now.) From 1343 Óbuda was the Queen's castle and the centre of her estates; Visegrád was not only a summer residence, but the Holy Crown was also kept here. Thus Visegrád had the same role as Karlstejn in Bohemia.

So in Hungary a central region was formed already in the Age of the House of Árpád, where the central functions were dealt with not in one settlement but in a region and within this several towns. Among them Buda was clearly the most important both as the capital and the royal residence. Buda — together with its sister town on the left bank of the Danube, Pest — was the economic centre of the country as well. All this had a very significant influence on the economic and cultural life of the whole country. The number of the staff of the royal household increased not only the market potentials of the merchants and craftsmen of the town, but also made it necessary to start enormous palace constructions. Even in the time of King Luis II (1516—1526), who was our poorest king and who always had financial difficulties, a household of 650 persons received salaries from the Treasury (not counting the priests of the royal chapel, the personnel and guards of the Buda castle and the household of the Queen). King Luis II was of Polish origin and he was the Bohemian king as well, so there were a number of Czechs, Polish and German people in the royal household in Buda. One part of the royal household stayed in Buda, even when the King left, though this did not often happen between 1523 and 1526. Most of the employees of the court lived in the castle; the others worked at the crown office, court of justice and Teasury and lived in the town.

A large number of noblemen travelled here from all parts of the country for the meetings of the Parliament and the regular judical sessions. They needed board and lodging and entertainment, which enriched the burghers. Many taverns and inns were opened in Buda, where a lot of musicians, mainly lute—players and violinists lived (this is proved by data).

Thus Buda can be considered as the melting pot of folk culture as people were able to hear and know the songs of other regions, which were sometimes influenced by the high—quality music life of the royal court. Our sovereigns invited to Buda not only outstanding foreign scholars, writers and artists but musicians as well. One of the court musicians of Queen Maria, the wife of Luis II was, for example, the famous German composer, Thomas Stolzer. Hungarian songs about heroic deeds in the Turkish battles were also performed in the royal court.

Now I only emphasized the importance of music in the central region, but it was certainly significant in other fields as well. Esztergom was also a literary and artistic centre thanks to the primates. In spite of the favourable conditions one factor was missing. Between 1440 and 1526 (when Luis II fell in the battle of Mohács), i.e. in 86 years there was a queen living in the Buda royal court only for 26 years. Mostly single or widowed kings lived in the castle. Thus the female members of the aristocracy did not visit the capital, though women played a very important role in popularizing culture during the Middle Ages. Beatrix of Aragon, the second wife of King Matthias, was an excellent example of this, who lived with Matthias for fourteen years (1476—1490). She was queen for the longest period, and — as it is well—known — cultural life developed enormously in our country.

ESZTERGOM

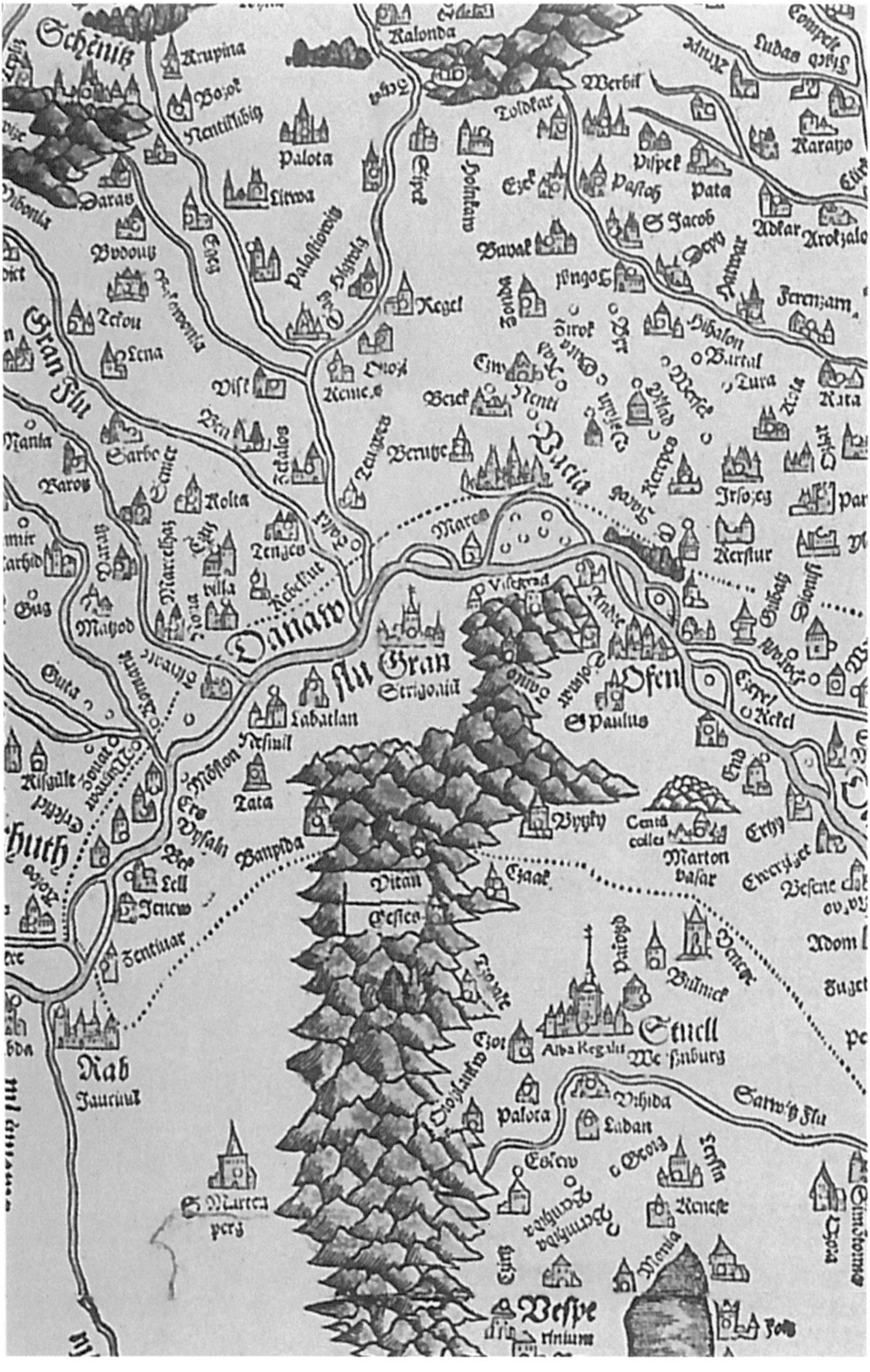

Schemitz
Krupina
Bozok
Nentdibih
Palota
Litwa
Saras
Budouiz
Tetou
Lena
Palastiowiz
Kegel
Enox
Reme
Vist
Mania
Baros
Sarbec
Tenec
Rolta
Tenges
Rebefhit
villa
Danaw
Gran Flu

Ralonda
Werbil
Toldkar
Vispek
Esck
Pastoh
Pata
Raravo
Bawal
S. Jacob
Adkar
Arokzalo
Ferenzam
Vhalon
Bartal
Tura
Rata
Beck
Nenti
Bernye
Lucia
Irsoies
par
Kerstur

Mares
Viskrad
Ofen
flu Gran
Strigonui
S. Paulus
Labatlan
Nesuil
Moson
Tata
Vysaly
Bampida
Vitan
Geslica
Cisak
Vyyky
Centu colles
Marton vasar
Erzij
Besene
Adom
Fuget

Stuell
Weisenburg
Alba Regalis
Bulnick
Bauer
Palota
Vhida
Laban
Esktu
Georg
Renest
Mania
Sartu Flu

Vespe
rinium

S. Marten
perg

Rab
Jaurinul

huth
Zentiuar
Genew
Gell
Jenew
Guta
Mayod
Gug

THE MEDIEVAL ESZTERGOM

From the foundation of the state to the beginning of the 13th century Esztergom was a royal seat, one of the centres of the political, economic and cultural life of the Árpádian Hungary. It was also the see of the archbishop, the head of the Hungarian church.

The importance of the settlement can be explained partly by the factors which facilitated the development of significant settlements in the place of the present town, parlty by the political situation of the 10th—12th centuries.

The favourable geographical conditions, first of all its location: being situated at the meeting point of hills and the plain (areas different in economy), in the 'line of market towns', near the waterway and ferry, with an area in the vicinity rich in waters and suitable for farming, greatly contributed to the development of the town. The former Roman road ('limes' road) and the River Garam and its valley meeting the Danube opposite the town meant good roads both on land and water. These roads crossed the road from the south—east along the Vörösvár—Dorog valley at Várhegy (castle hill), where one of the most important ferries of the area was to be found. It was easy to control this junction important both from military and commercial points of view, from Várhegy rising right above the ferry.

So a fortress was built already in the Celtic then the Roman times on the top of the hill with a settlement below which — as sources say — played an important role in the commerce of the neighbouring area as well.

The Avars and later the conquering Hungarians as well recognized the military and commercial importance of the place. This is suggested by the archaelogical finds uncovered in the town and its vicinity. Besides them — similarly to other settlements in Pannonia — there must have been the remains of significant Roman buildings; so it is very probable that Prince Géza formed his fortified residencial palace here using the remains of the former Roman 'castrum'. As Esztergom was on the road leading to the west, it was also a favourable scene for Prince Géza to build up relations with the western countries. In 973 the legates of Prince Géza left from here for Quedlinburg, to the court of Emperor Otto, to offer peace to finish the former wars and ask for missionaries. The missionaries who built the first Christian church in honour of the St. Stephen the Martyr on Várhegy beside the palace of Prince Géza were also received here.

Between 969—975 Géza's son, Vajk, was born and christened Stephen (together with his father) here. In 995 the Prince's court was also visited by the bishop of Prague, who was later martyred, then was canonized.

Together with the missionaries merchants also arrived in Esztergom, which — defended by the castle of the Prince — was becoming to be a commercial and industrial centre. According to the lastest research the Hungarian name of the town also originated in this early period. It refers to the work of the Bulgarian—Turkish craftsmen who made leather armour for the army of the Prince (Estrogen — estrigin, respectively esztrogin: leather armour maker — Esztrigon — Esztergom).

St. Stephen was crowned king here on 1 January 1001; and in the same year he founded the Esztergom archdiocene, which became the head of the ten Hungarian bishoprics organized by him.

From then on Esztergom was not only a royal centre but an ecclesiastical centre and the seat of the county situated on the two banks of the Danube. (First the county was governed by bailiffs, from 1270 the archbishops were the bailiffs as well.)

During the 11th—12th centuries the most monumental secular and ecclesiactical building complex (including the royal palace, the palace of the archbishop, the cathedral, chapter house, etc.) of the Árpádian Hungary was developed on Várhegy. Protected by the castle near the Little—Danube, one of the most significant towns of the country developed here from the settlements of the servants of the court of the prince, later of the king, and those of craftsmen and merchants already at the end of the 10th century. From among the Hungarian towns Esztergom owned staple rights first, which meant that under royal orders every merchant trading at great distances had to come here and offer their goods for sale. The goods transported by land were imposed duty on at the ferry of Esztergom—Kakat (today Kakat is Párkány on the other side of the Danube) as well as at the market place of the town. The main harbour of merchant ships was on the Little—Danube, as it never froze over because of the hot water springs there. The richest people of the town were among the merchants who were of western origin, trading at great distances, and among the several craftsmen.

Both the royal castle and the industrial-commercial town under it were big and European in manners and exterior. The foreign kings visited the Hungarian kings here: e.g. in 1147 Luis VII, French king visited Géza II (a friar, Odo de Deogilo, travelling in the retinue of the king writes: '... the Danube collects the treasure and wealth of several countries in the famous Esztergom...'); in 1172 Lion (Welf) Henry, Bavarian and Saxon prince and Henry (Jasomirgott) II, Austrian prince visited Stephen III. In 1189 Frederick Barbarossa and his crusaders were received here by Béla III and Queen Margaret with royal pomp and then the Emperor was richly presented. In his description Arnold of Lübeck travelling with the army of the Emperor called Esztergom the capital of the Hungarians ('...when the Emperor arrived in the town which is called Gran,' — Gran is the German name of Esztergom — 'which is the capital of the Hungarians...' — 'que Ungerorum est... Metropolis').

The royal palace and St. Adalbert's Cathedral destroyed in a blaze in the 1180s were rebuilt at this time. The town consisting of a conglomeration of settlements was already lying on a larger area than today's Esztergom. This flourishing place was destoyed, most of its inhabitants killed by the Mongols in January—February 1242 — as the witness Master Rogerius, the canon of Nagyvárad described. They were, however, not able to occupy the royal castle defended by the archers of bailiff Simon.

The Mongol invasion wrecked the development of Esztergom. Though the town was soon rebuilt, King Béla IV moved the royal seat to Buda and, worried about another attack of the Mongols, transferred the rich burghers of the town in the north part of the castle (1249). Later, after the danger was over, and also because of the frictions between the burghers and clergymen, the burghers moved back to the royal town, and the king bestowed the royal palace upon the archbishop (1256).

After this only the 'Royal Town' surrounded with ramparts and ditches and the suburb, 'Kovácsi' in the south—east were under the authority of the king (though the church acquired quite large estates here as well). The castle, Viziváros (Érsekváros or Újváros) — Waterside town (Archbishop's town or Newtown) — and most of the suburbs were under the authority of the church in the Middle Ages; and the burghers of the royal town fought long battles to keep their rights.

Several ecclesiastical institutions and religious orders settled down in the ecclesiastical centre. Up to the 15th century we have data about 11 friaries, convents and monasteries and altogether 38 churches in the town and settlements belonging to it and built in its direct vicinity. The formers were important centres of the medieval education, culture and artistc life: besides the college of the cathedral chapter in the castle, the order of the Austin Hermits also had a college in the St.Anna quarter; the Dominicans and Franciscans owned significant schools as well. Famous personalies like Pelbárt Temesvári and Osvát Laskai taught in the latter.

The commercial importance of the town gradually decreased after the Mongol invasion, though the burghers did everything to keep their privileges.

The decrease of the turnover and money circulation were paralleled with the strengthening of the new capital, Buda. One of the factors of this procedure was that the only mint from St. Stephen's period to the beginning of the 13th century, after the Buda mint was established in 1255, gradually ceased to function; though it still worked under the control the Buda mint for some time, it closed down by the middle of the 14th century.

In spite of the fact that it had lost its secular importance, Esztergom still played a role of national significance, first of all owing to the archbishops and the cathedral chapter.

The archbishops of Esztergom were generally royal chancellors as well. Our kings and their noted guests were often entertained in the Esztergom castle, which was already enlarged by the archbishops. Csanád Telegdy (1330 —1349) was the first who brought about considerable changes: besides enlarging the royal palace and rebuilding the cathedral, he built fortification and renewed its churches in Viziváros. In the 15th century Dénes Széchy (1440—1465), János Vitéz (1465—1472) and Hippolit Estei (1487—1497), enlightened prelates, were outstanding patrons and builders. Due to them the much admired, huge, late Gothic palace and great hall were built and St. Adalbert's basilica was enlarged and rebuilt; and the palace in the Esztergom castle matched up with the royal palaces in Buda and Visegrád.

Their work was continued by Archbishop Tamás Bakócz already in Renaissance style; he constructed the most gorgeous building of the Hungarian Renaissance architecture, the Bakócz chapel, which has remained to us.

At the same time the court of the archbishop of Esztergom equalled the royal court not only in architecture but in supporting and practising arts and sciences as well.

Writers, painters, sculptors, bell-founders and goldsmiths worked in the castle and in the town.

After the death of King Matthias, in the time of Tamás Bakócz (1497—1521) and György Szathmáry (1521—1524), the court of the archbishop of Esztergom took the lead not only in supporting sciences and arts but also in pomp before the declining Buda royal court. This development was interrupted by the Mohács defeat (29 August 1526), in which László Szalkai, the Archbishop of Esztergom, at the head of his 1,500 hussars was killed, similarly to his predecessor, who died in the Mongol invasion. In less than two weeks the raiding Turkish troops ransacked and burnt the town of Esztergom. The castle was endangered, too, as András Orbánczi, the caSt...ellan, left the town after he had pilfered the ships of the Queen fleeing from Buda. Lieutenant Máté Nagy, who escaped from the Mohács battle, succeeded in defending the castle with his few soldiers and the people fleeing there, against the Tukish siege. Owing to its important strategical place the Esztergom castle, however, could not avoid its fate: it was occupied by Sultan Suleiman in 1543. It was a Turkish border castle till 1683, except for ten years (1595—1605), altogether for 130 years. The castle, which was on the border of the part of the country under Turkish rule and the royal Hungary, i.e. in the way of the Turkish attacks against northern Hungary and Vienna, respectively those trying to free Buda, had to face several devastating sieges. So the medieval settlement so famous for its buildings was completely ruined; nothing remained beyond the ramparts of the castle and Viziváros after the Turks had been expelled. On the place of the demolished ruins, on new foundations, with new plans a new town was built.

1. VÁRHEGY. Medieval legend has it that on top of the hill above the ferry.

THE TOPOGRAPHY OF THE MEDIEVAL ESZTERGOM:

The core of Esztergom was formed by three parts protected by the castle, ramparts and ditches.

1. the royal, later archbishopric castle on Várhegy,
2. the town of the archbishop, also called Viziváros — between Várhegy and the Danube,
3. the royal town about 300 m to the south—east of Várhegy on the bank of the Little—Danube.

These three fortified settlements — similarly to other towns of the Árpádian age — were surrounded by smaller or larger settlements. The medieval Esztergom was formed by a conglomerate of districts generally built together, belonging to different owners (the king, the archbishop, cathedral chapter, religious orders, secular persons); these districts had separate names, e.g. St. Anna quarter — Contratra Sancte Anne, Kovácsi, Újfalu, etc. The suburbs may have been settlements on larger areas, with a loose structure and with only

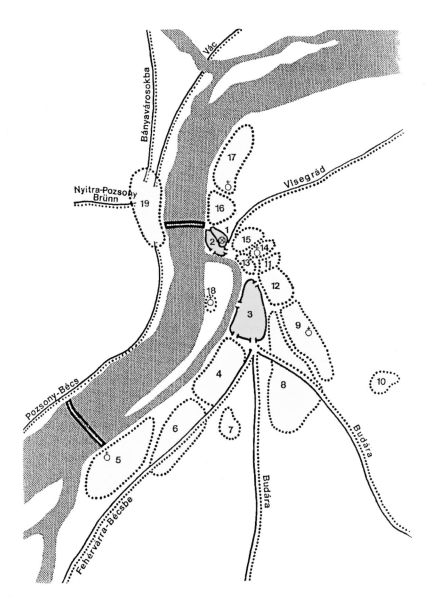

a few significant buildings (churches, friaries, etc.). This explains that the town spread on a much larger area than today's Esztergom, mainly in the south, south—west and north.
The suburbs built together with the core of the town were:
4. St. Paul; 5. Abony—Szentkirály; 6. St. Stephen; 7. St. Lazarus; 8. Kovácsi; 9. Újfalu; 11. Örmény; 12. St. Anna quarter; 13. Héviz or Tapolca; 14. St. Thomas; 15. Libád; 16. Petény; 17. St. George; 18. the Island; 19. Kakat.
A little further on were the settlements belonging to the town:
10. *Fenyérd and Bylle; Bajon; Peszér; Urkuta; Ákospalota and Zamárd.*

VÁRHEGY

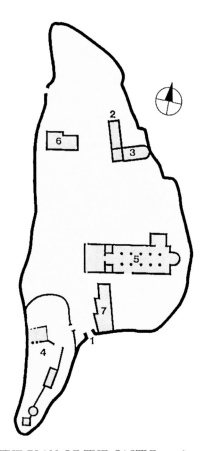

THE PLAN OF THE CASTLE, *11th century*

'...before the time of King Stephen ... his father (King) Géza started to build the Esztergom castle , too, ...' says the canonica visitatio in 1397. The first walls of the castle followed the upper, irregular, oval edge of the hill. The main buildings of the castle were built in the 10th—11th centuries. The gate opened in the south—east, on the gentle slope of the hill (1). Medieval legend has it that the palace of Prince Géza was built on the north side of the hill (2), where King Stephen was born between 969 and 975. The church of St. Stephen the Martyr was situated beside it, it was built by the first missionaries (3). The new palace of King Stephen was built on the southern top of the hill (4); after the foundation of the archdiocene, in 1001 he built the arch-bishopric cathedral in honour of the Virgin Mary and St. Adalbert in the middle of the hilltop (5). The palace of the archbishop was built on the north—western side of the hill in the 11th—12th centuries (6), the monastery of the cathedral chapter (the residence of the canons) on the south side of St. Adalbert's church (7).

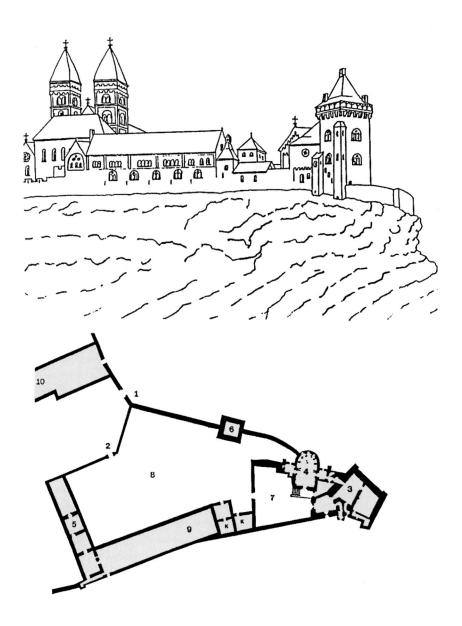

THE RECONSTRUCTION AND PLAN OF THE ESZTERGOM PALACE OF THE
KINGS OF THE HOUSE OF ÁRPÁD *from the north, the end of the 12th century*

The buildings of the castle were destroyed in a blaze in the 1180s. The shape
of the castle was decided by the construction work of King Béla III (1172—1196)
and Archbishop Jób. The biggest secular building complex of the Árpádian age,
the new royal palace was built then. Its plan is quite exactly known from the

archaelogical research of the recent years. The palace standing on the south, rocky stretch of the hill was built 130 m in length in north—southern direction around a triangular courtyard, thus forming another fortress within the castle.

The gate in the south—east was the common entrance of the royal and arch-bishopric castle. To the west an inner curtain wall closed the palace from the bailey, from where the gate 2 led to the outer ward of the palace (8). The keep, called 'Fehér Torony' (white tower) was accessible through the gate of the

THE REMAINS OF THE PALACE OF THE KINGS OF THE HOUSE OF ÁRPÁD *from Víziváros*

inner ward (7). It was standing on the top of the southern cliff and was the most protected building of the palace.

The multi—storey keep was the residential building of the royal family (3). The royal chapel (4) was situated on its north side; it was one of the master pieces of late Romanesque — early Gothic architecture, the style of which refer to French contacts. The remains of the church ruined in the Turkish times were uncovered and reconstructed between 1934 and 1938. During the excavations in the 1930s

THE KEEP

Double portal   *Part of the 'St. Stephen's Hall'*

THE ROYAL CHAPEL IN THE CASTLE

A PART OF THE CASTLE CHAPEL

THE FACADE OF THE CASTLE CHAPEL WITH THE FAMOUS ROSE—WINDOW

only the remains of the southern palace and some parts of the northern palace (5) were found; there was an attempt made to reconstruct the residential building of Béla III. The remains found lately completely changed the conception: according to them the southern finds were only parts of the royal apartment, which was protected by an small inner yard. The actual royal palace (palacium magnum — big palace) was the building standing on the Danube side of the outer ward in the direction of the north — north—west and south — south—east; it was 50 m long and 10 m wide (9); its complete lower level and significant parts of the upper level have remained. The latter, which was one 45 m long hall with five big recesses towards the Danube must have been the thone room.

In the north, the big palace was built to a two—level wing, the north palace (5, guest rooms?) consisting of several rooms. In the east, the huge ward was protected with tall ramparts and a big, square tower (6).

THE PALACE OF ARCHBISHOP VITÉZ

After the royal court moved from here, the 'big palace' (9) was rebuilt in Gothic style by Csanád Telegdy, then rebuilt and enlarged by archbishops Dénes Széchy (1440—1465) and János Vitéz (1465—1472).

Dénes Széchy started the construction work taking pattern of the Palace of King Sigismund in Buda and the new palace of the Hunyadi's in Vajdahunyad. To the west (Danube) side of the big palace another wing of the same size was built; on the upper level a spacious grand hall was created, owing to its size (47 m long, 16.5 m wide) it must have been one of largest halls of the con-

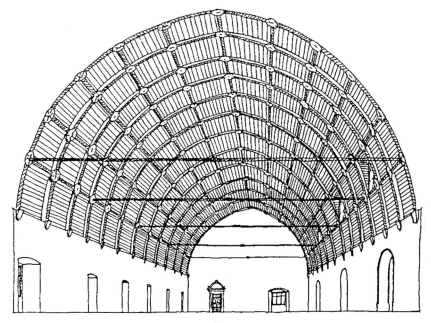

THE HALL OF THE VITÉZ PALACE, *reconstruction*

THE VIEW OF THE VITÉZ PALACE FROM THE DANUBE, *reconstruction* (*by I. Horváth*)

temporary Hungary. The famous Sibyl Chapel opened from the north—western end of the big hall; outside the western facade of the hall between the bay windows standing on buttresses a balcony passageway on supports was built. Bonfini (the historiographer of King Matthias) writes the following about this palace: '.... He (János Vitéz built a spacious dining hall in the castle, and beside it a splendid red marble two—level balcony passageway. Outside the facade of the hall a vaulted and gable—roofed chapel was erected, in which the pictures of all the sibyls can be seen. In the hall not only all the Hungarian kings are depicted in chronological order but the Scythian ancestors as well'.

The palace much admired and described by contemporaries was destroyed in the Turkish times (1595). Significant remains have been found in recent years, which and the results of further research may make it possible to recontruct the Vitéz palace and the big hall in the near future.

THE FACADE OF THE VITÉZ PALACE FROM THE YARD, *reconstruction*

ST. ADALBERT'S CHURCH

According to some sources the construction work started in 1010, but it is more probable that King Stephen began to build the archbishopric cathedral in honour of St. Adalbert on the highest point of Várhegy at the same time with the foundation of the archdiocese (1001). In 1156 Archbishop Martirius established the altar of the Blessed Virgin Mary in it. King Stephen III was buried here in 1172.

Between 1185 and 1188 the church was destroyed in a blaze. The ruined building was rebuilt by King Béla III and Archbishop Jób. It became damaged again when in 1304 Wenceslas, Bohemian king occupied the castle, broke into the cathedral and plundered the Treasury and record office. At the beginning of the 14th century the reconstruction work started again, and it was only finished by Csanád Telegdy (1330—1349). The chronicle writes about him: '... he had the chancel rebuilt from its foundations from carved and polished stones, with wonderfully ornamented pillars, strong plinths, beautifully formed beams and splendid vaulting, and finished it with glazed windows and fortification from the outside. He equipped the church with gilt tables of kiss of peace, cups and jewelry...'

In 1385 Archbishop Demeter built a side chapel to the south side, in 1396 János Kanizsai to the north side. The next rebuilding of the church was during the time of Archbishop Dénes Széchy, who consecrated the basilica to the Blessed Virgin Mary and St. Adalbert in 1453. Soon Archbishop János Vitéz furbished the church, too, (1465—1472): he built a steeper roof, with coloured glazed tiles, and to the north side a two—level library.

In 1506—1507 to the southern side of the church Tamás Bakócz (+1521) built his own sepulchral chapel, which surviving the Turkish wars is the most beautiful, intact masterpiece of the Renaissance architecture in Hungary. The devastation of the church started in 1543, when Sultan Suleiman besieged and occupied the Esztergom castle. The remains of the church destroyed in the Turkish wars were pulled down after a careful suvey and before the new basilica was built. We only know some 16th—century perspective drawings, some stone carvings and the plan of the 'Magnificent Church' of the medieval Hungary (Ecclesia Magnifica).

In the etching made before the devastation in 1595 most of St. Adalbert's Church is still intact but its chancel is destroyed.
(by an unknown artist)

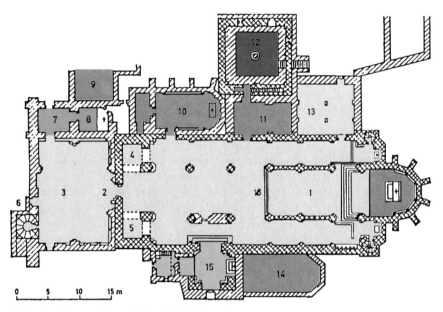

THE PLAN OF ST. ADALBERT'S CHURCH *(after János Máthes)*

THE EXPLANATION OF THE PLAN:

1. The choir, which was three steps higher than the nave. The stalls of the canons stood here. From here five steps led to the main chancel, which was buttressed and closed with the sides of a polygon, and which was built by Csanád Telegdy in the 14th century. The apse may originally have been semicircular.

2. The western portal of the church, the famous Porta Speciosa (beautiful portal), which was built by King Béla III and Archbishop Jób after the blaze, between 1188 and 1196. It was a porch with red and white marble jamb arches and ornamented with incrusted pictures of coloured marble in a red marble basis. On both sides of the porch, the pillars of semicircular niches stood on red marble lions and white marble crouching figures. In the niches there were three prophets on both sides, on the door—posts incrusted pictures of evangelists and local saints, in their hands ribbons with inscriptions from the Bible. In the tympanum King St. Stephen offered Hungary in the patronage of the Virgin Mary, to the left stood the fig-

ure of St. Adalbert. On the ledger of the porch the kneeling figures of King Béla III and Archbishop Jób were to be seen. The porch destroyed in the 18th century can be reconstructed on the basis of a contemporary painting, description and the original fragments.

3. The covered, vaulted, probably two—level vestibule built in the 12th—13th centuries, its main entrance opened from the south.

4. The northern of the two towers on the western facade. On the ground floor was St. Jeremy's Chapel, which was founded by Canon Mihály Kesztölci in 1499.

5. The southern tower on the ground floor of which was St. Andrew's Chapel founded by Canon András Pápai in 1495.

6. The tower of the spiral staircase leading from the ground floor of the vestibule to the first floor. In 1543 Sultan Suleiman built a minaret on it.

7. The northern small vestibule, which was St. Lucy's Chapel with a crypt under it. It already existed in the 13th century.

8. The Holy Trinity Chapel with the altar of the same name. It already existed in 1397.

'PORTA SPECIOSA' (BEAUTIFUL PORTAL) — *model*

9. The walls of the flat of the guard canon.

10. The Chapel and sacristy of the Blessed Virgin Mary. It was founded by Archbishop—Chancellor János Kanizsay in 1396. In 1496 an organ was built in it.

11. The Chapel of the Holy Sacrament. It already existed in 1391.

12. The library of Archbishop János Vitéz. It was accessible from the church through the chapel. It consisted of of a ground—floor hall vaulted on a middle pillar above a cellar, and a first—floor hall which was accessible on a narrow staircase in the southern wall.

13. The sacristy and treasury (and record office) — the council room of the chapter as well, built to the north—eastern end of the aisle.

14. The Corpus Christi Chapel founded by Archbishop Demeter in 1384.

15. Maria Annunciata Chapel — erected by Archbishop Tamás Bakócz in 1506 as his own burial place. According to Jolán Balogh the highly ornamented red marble Renaissance chapel was built by an architect of Tuscan origin, belonging to the group of Giulio de Sangallo and Salvi d'Andrea.

We have written sources about ten altars in the church. Besides St. Adalbert's altar in the main chancel, now we only mention the altar of the Holy Cross, the so—called 'Népoltár' (people's altar) (16), which stood in front of the choir. It already existed before 1397.

Its rector altaris was the parson of the castle.

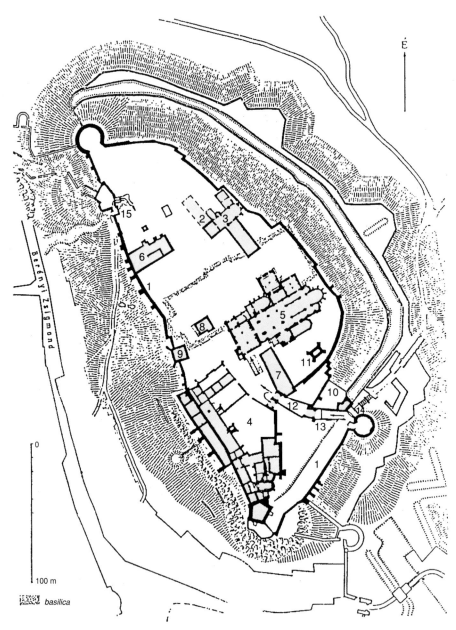

THE PLAN OF THE MEDIEVAL BUILDINGS OF THE CASTLE
based on surveys and excavations

(Some significant architectural remains of the destroyed church can be found in the collection of the castle museum; and a large number of stone carvings from the chancel were found during the excavations in 1983—1984.)

The palace of the archbishops (6). The place of the palace of the archbishops in the Árpádian age are mentioned in the 1249 and 1256 charters of King Béla IV: it was situated in the 'big castle', beside the western ramparts, north of the royal palace. Its exact location was determined by László Zolnay's excavation in 1957. It was a 15 m x 35 m building, with a western—eastern axis, its western facade was supported by the ramparts on the Danube side.

The last rebuilding was completed by Archbishop Bakócz between 1497 and 1500, when it was the residential palace of the archbishop again during the Esztergom stay of Queen Beatrix (1490—1500). The building rebuilt in the 18th century as well was pulled down in 1821.

Chapter house — monastery (Monasterium Sancti Adalberti — 7). The cathedral chapter developed gradually after the foundation of the archdiocese (1001) by the end of the 11th century from the priests of the cathedral. Its members, the canons (Benedictine monks in the early period) still lived a monastic life in the Árpádian age. From the 13th century, when the canons had a house of their own outside the castle or as part of their prebend, the monastery still remained the centre of the chapter. The Esztergom chapter was one of the most significant ecclesiastical bodies entrusted with notorial funtions, which is proved by several hundred charters written here.

The building of the monastery used for military purposes in the 16th—18th centuries was pulled down in 1822.

The house of the provost (8). The house of the provost heading the chapter — according to a charter of King Béla IV, written in 1249 — stood between the chapter house and the palace of the archbishop. In the 18th century this building was the house of the castellan; it was pulled down during some earthwork between 1762 and 1763.

THE TOWERS:

In the 14th—15th centuries the ramparts were fortified with new towers. Contemporary sources mention that e.g. Archbishop Csanád Telegdy ' ... renovated the ramparts and towers of the castle, which began to decay because they were old and not taken care of, and built several new tall and strong towers to strenghen the castle.' The tower which was uncovered on the western rampart by István Méri in 1961 may have been one of them; it was fortified with buttresses, its size was 7 m x 8 m inside and its foundation was 3 m wide (9); the findings date it at the 14th or15th century.

During some earthwork in the 19th century the walls of a square tower with buttresses were pulled down on the south side of the old church (11); up to recent years it was considered to be a Roman watch—tower on the basis of the nearby findings. This tower, which was the tallest in the medieval castle, was built by Archbishop Tamás Bakócz after 1499 'to guard and protect the whole castle' and the cathedral. It can be seen in 16th century etchings as well. The tower was destroyed in the Turkish wars.

THE GATES:

The gate of the Árpádian upper castle was reconstructed to be a double gate after the outer south—eastern protecting system was built to provide access for the latter (12). In front of the old gate a machicolated parapet was built with a defile in the 14th century, which was accessible through the middle gatehouse and the drawbridge across the pitfall outside it (13). In front of it the outer defile was to be found with an outer gate beside the Buda Tower, which was accessible across a wooden bridge over the outer ditch, with a drawbridge and a pitfall outside the gate (14). Most of the latter two can still be seen today as well; the inner gate was pulled down in 1821—1822, and partly restored in 1993—1994.

Towards Viziváros the castle had a gate only for pedestrians: the Viziváros Gate, also called 'cat's walk' gate (15).

This was the name of the stairs leading up the steep hillside from Viziváros. Evilia Celebi says the following about the 'small gate opening into the outer castle': '... It is a path leading down to the suburb, no horse can go it, it is difficult to walk on even for a man. It is of five hundred stairs made by Hungarians'.

Most of the medieval buildings of the castle were destroyed and ruined in the Turkish wars.

The remains were either pulled down or buried during the earthwork before the today's basilica was built.

VÍZIVÁROS:

At the foot of Várhegy, the area between the hill and the banks of the Danube and the Little—Danube, on the north and south end of which there are thermal springs abounding in water, belonged to the archbishop and inhibited by his serfs already before the 13th century. In 1239 King Béla IV allowed Archbishop Robert to found a town here to protect his church and serfs.

The town spread from the thermal springs flowing into the Little—Danube (near the today's Mattyasovszky bastion) as far as a tower in the north, called Veprech (at 20 Berényi Zs. utca) along the bank of the Danube.

Besides the weekly market from Fiday midday to Saturday evening the king invested the new town with other rights as well without prejudice to the rights of the royal town and its market.

This town must already have been protected by some palisade at the time of the Mongol invasion. The stone ramparts (most of which can still be seen in a rebuilt shape) were constructed by Archbishop Csanád Telegdy in the first half of the 14th century: '... he made the town adjacent to the castle safe and strong, fortified it with thick walls and strong towers...'.

The narrow area between the foot of the hill and the Danube was densely built up in the Middle Ages. Besides the construction work of the burghers, the

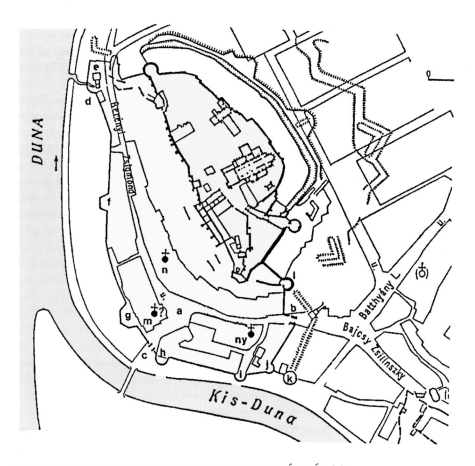

THE PLAN OF THE ESZTERGOM CASTLE AND VÍZIVÁROS

building of Archbishops János Kanizsay and János Vitéz was of great significance as well.

The market place of the town was in the square in front of the today's two—
towered church (a), from where roads led to three towngates: one to the Buda
Gate — this was (and still is) the main street of Viziváros; the second to the
Vizi Gate (water gate) — from here a wooden bridge led onto the island over
the Little—Danube; and the third to the Kis Gate (small gate) to the northern
end of the town (this was the other stretch of the main street). Here only a
pedestrian gate opened to the Danube, to the nearby ferry, respectively to
Szentgyörgymező.

The forth street of Viziváros was between the Vizi Gate and the Buda Gate
between the southern rampart and the main street, parallel to the rampart. (This
street, called Szt. János utca in the last century, was built up in the 1920s. Its
south—eastern end has remained: today Katona István utca.)

The most important medieval buildings of this small town: the tower of the Buda Gate (b) — it opened to the east in front of the building at 55 of today's Bajcsi Zsilinszky út. It was pulled down at the end of the 18th century.

The tower of Vizi Gate (c) also called Rév Gate (ferry gate) — it was in the middle of the road between Szt. István (St. Stephen) Grammar School and the gate of the Primás—kert (primate's garden); it was pulled down in 1815.

The Kis Gate (d) at the northern end of Viziváros. It was rebuilt by the Turks, this building can be seen today. Veprech tower and Malom (mill) bastion (e). The archbishop's Vizi Gate was already mentioned in 1239 as being near the thermal springs at the northern feet of Várhegy. The tower, which ensured the water supply of the castle and protected the water mill beside it, mentioned already in the 14th century, played a very important role in the defence system of the castle. It was joined to the castle with walls on the hillside; and forming a separate fortress together with the Malom bastion in Viziváros, it had separate castellans already in the 15th century. The watermill of the Árpádian age was recontructed into a water—wheel which pushed the water from the Danube up to the castle at the end of the 15th century. This water—wheel is described by György Wernher before 1551 as follows: ' ... at the bank of the Danube the thermal spring is enclosed in a tower where a passage leads between the steep walls from the castle. This spring is so abundant in water that it drives a wheat grinding mill and now a drum—like bucket—wheel as well, which immerses into the water of the Danube in an underground canal under the tower and pushes the water up to the castle.'

The Malom bastion of old Italian type, ensuring better defence to the water—wheel was built by Archbishop Pál Váradi in 1543. On the western rampart of Víziváros there were two bastions, too, (f—g); they must have been built still before the Turkish occupation, the semicircular and circular bastions (h—l), however, were already built by the Turks in the 16th—17th centuries.

There is data about three medieval churches in Viziváros: the present parish building (3. Berényi út) and two churches in the place of the parish church (m—n); neither the date of their construction, nor their patron saints are known. It is only certain that the previous was rebuilt into a mosque by the Turks.

The parish church of the town was situated in the place of the present convent church, and it was consecrated in honour of St. Ladislas (ny). It may have been founded in the Árpádian period; it was often mentioned in 14th—15th century charters; it was still dipiced in 1959, so it must have been destroyed later. ·

Besides the above, there is written data about several secular buildings, but the remains of only a few can still be seen.

THE ROYAL TOWN — The medieval royal town developed on the bank of the Little—Danube, in the protection of the castle of the prince in the second half of the 10th century. The slightly rolling territory of the town, separated like an island, was bordered in the north and south by ditches formed by water from the hills and in the east by the old, silted branch of the Danube.

In the age of the foundation of the state, the whole area was still the estate of the king; its northern quarter gradually got in the hands of the Church in the 12th—13th centuries. The northern part of the settlement which from the 11th century was defended with ditches, then with palisades, from the 13th century with ramparts (1), was the quarter of the royal household. It was also called St. Lawrence quarter named after St. Lawrence's parish church (7) beside

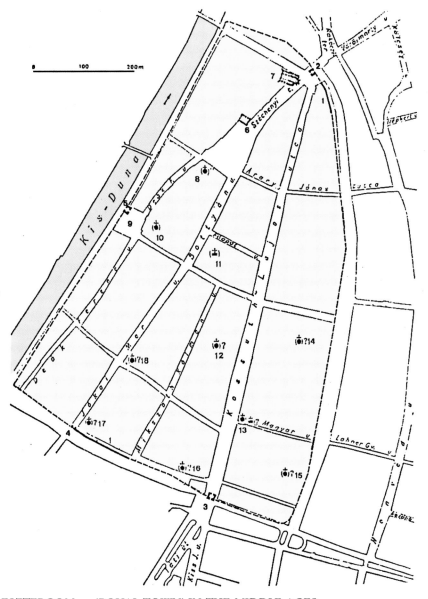

ESZTERGOM — 'ROYAL TOWN' IN THE MIDDLE AGES

the St. Lawrence Gate opening in the north (2). The big market place of the quarter was situated in the south, around today's Széchenyi tér; it was the most significant commercial centre of the Árpádian Hungary. In the Middle Ages the town hall and — where the square widens — the most important Árpádian mint (6) were situated here. In the south—western side of the square was the parish curch consecrated in honour of St. Nicholas, the patron saint of merchants (8), which separated the main square from the fish market (9) to the south—west of it spreading to the Vizi Gate by the Little—Danube (5).

The bigger, southern part of the town had several districts which generally developed around a parish church. The Latin quarter was adjacent to the southern side of the market place.

The 'Latiners', the richest burghers of Belgian, French, Wallon and Italian (i.e. Latin) origin, dealing mainly with long—distance goods traffic and crafts-manship (goldsmithery) lived here. The members of the town council were also chosen from them; they were given the right to issue sealed charters by Andrew II (1205—1235). The market—halls of these merchants — as men-tioned in contemporary charters — were on the south side of the square and in the streets leading here. Their parish church must have been St. Peter's Church named after the patron saint of different crafts (10). To the east was the church and friary of the Franciscans, named after the Helping Virgin Mary, this was the second biggest church in the town. King Béla IV and his family were buried here under an ornamented red marble tomb.

The quarter of the Jews was around the synagogue to the south—east of the quarter of the 'Latins', there are data available about them already from the beginning of the 11th century. Their cemetery, however, was not around the church (12), but to the south, outside the ramparts.

There are very few data about the south part of the town. There were several churches here, too, with smaller quarters named after their churches. The place of the church, convent and hospice of the Hospitallers of St. John of Jerusalem, called the Holy Cross, can be identified in the vicinity the today's Rácz Church (13). It is only the places of the other churches (of St. James, Mary Magdalen, St. Giles, the church and convent of the Templars and a church whose name is unknown) that is roughly known from archaelogical finds (14—18); it will only be possible to identify them with charter data when they are excavated. The place of St. Paul Gate is exactly known (4); it opened to the south—west in the line of Jókai utca and the road through it led across a wooden bridge over the moat to the Szentpál (St. Paul) quarter. In the south part of the town as charters say and archaelogical finds show, all kinds of craftsmen (smiths, butchers, cobblers, tailors, tanners, etc.) lived, some of whom also had farms, but most of the burghers dealt with wine—growing on the eastern hillsides. The medieval royal town was completely ruined in the Turkish wars. Archaelogical data show that its network of streets was entirely different from the that of the new town. The market place (main square) and the fish market, however, were situated in the place of the present Széchenyi tér and Pór Antal tér, but they are supposed to have been much more extensive than today.

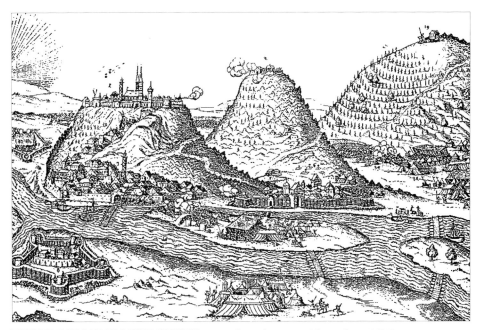

ESZTERGOM FROM THE SOUTH — *etching by Hans Sibmacher, 1595*

THOMAS BACOTZ DE ERDEVD, CAR
DINALIS STRIGONIENSIS, ALMAE
DEI GENITRICI MARIAE VIRGINI
EXTRVXIT. ANNO M.D.VII.

STRIGONIVM. GRAN.

THE RUINS OF THE ROYAL TOWN — *part of the etching by Georg Houfnagel, 1595*

Written sources and relics prove that the area within the ramparts was densely built up. The significant buildings were mainly in the north of the town; the materials used were stone, bricks, adobe and wood.

Very good pictures remained about the royal town from the Turkish times. The etching by Hann Sibmacher gives a very good view of the still intact town from the south, and that by G. Houfnagel from the north after the destruction of the siege in 1595.

The royal town was encircled by suburbs. From the south—west

4. Szentpál joined to it. Archaelogical data prove that the settlement was continuously inhabited from the 9th—10th centuries. It was first recorded in a charter in 1236. From then on it was often mentioned in written sources up to the Turkish invasion. The owners were private persons, the archbishop, the chapter and the hospitalles from Szentkirály. The parish church was built in honour of St. Paul, it already existed before the Mongol invasion. To the south—west of Szentpál on the bank of the Danube lay

5. Szentkirály (Holy King=St. Stephen), which was originally called Abony (Obon). The remains of the parish church built in honour of St. Andrew at the biginning of the 11th century, with a chancel enclosed in a straight line outside and semicircularly inside, and the graves of the cemetery from the 11th—13th centuries were excavated between 1967 and 1981 together with some remains for the Árpádian age (parts of houses, ovens, ditches, etc.) Near the parish church, on the bank of the Danube, King Géza II built a three—aisled, double—towered church for the Hospitallers of the Order of St. Stephen; and consecrated it in honour of St. Stephen in the 1150s. The convent and hospice standing beside it was the centre of the independent Hungarian Order of the Hospitallers; and it was entrusted with notorial functions. The name of the settlement was changed from Abony to Szentkirály after the name of the patron saint of the church. The Hospitallers also controlled the ferry on the Danube at Szentkirály. This settlement was completely ruined in the Turkish times; its name remained in 'Szentkirályi dülő' (Holy King balk). On the road to Székesfehérvár between Szentkirály and Szentpál was

6. Szentistván—falva (St. Stephen's village), which received its name from its parish church named after the first martyr, St. Stephen. This settlement was united Szentkirály in the 13th—14th centuries. In the east in the vicinity of Szentistván and Szentpál lay

7. Szent Lázár (St. Lazarus). In the middle of the settlement stood St. Lazarus' church and hospice, which — as chronilces say — were founded by King Stephen ordering in their service the descendants of the soldiers beaten in the Ausburg siege.

Later the church and hospice were in the hands of the Hospitallers of Szentkirály, and destroyed in 16th century. To the east of Szent Lázár stretched as far as the royal town the largest medieval suburb of Esztergom

8. Kovácsi (kovács=smith). The settlement flourishing already in the 9th—10th centuries received its name from the smiths and other craftsmen working here. Rich archaelogical finds excavated near the Railway Station inform about its early period. Charters from the Árpádian age already mention three churches here

(St. Michael, St. John and St. Cosma—Damian). One of them (its ruins can be seen near the Railway Station) was surely built in the age of King Stephen. Under the church a furnace used for melting silver, bronze and tin, in the church a grave dated with the denarius of St. Stephen have been found. Esztergom was the centre of coin making from the 11th century; the minters lived here in Kovácsi (in the 11th century the mint worked in the castle, in the 12th—14th centuries already in the royal town). In 1264 King Béla IV bestowed the northern third of Kovácsi stretching as far as the royal town on the Premonstratensian monastery of Csut, so this part was also called the village of the Csut monastery.

In 1326 King Charles Robert attached the larger part of Kovácsi to the royal town, which together with this part was under the control of the king till the devastation of the Turks (it was in pawn of Tamás Bakócz, together with the royal town, between 1502 and 1519).

The present town settled in the place of the destroyed Kovácsi in the 19th—20th centuries. The eastern neighbour of Kovácsi was

9. Újfalu (new village) (Nova—Villa), the main building of which was St. Dominic's Church and the friary of the Dominicans, which already stood there in 1231. Friar Julianus, who visited the Hungarians remaining near the Ural, lived in this friary. The medieval relics of Újfalu have been found in a large area at the foot of the hill.

To the north of Újfalu between the Royal town, the hillside and Szenttamás Hill lay Örmény and Szent Anna (St. Anna's) quarter.

11. Örmény was the settlement of the Armenian merchants and craftsmen before the Mongol invasion. Their parish church, which was somewhere around today's Esze Tamás utca, was built in honour of St. John the Baptist. The privileged Armenian merchants of the quarter were exempt from duty in the whole country. They lost their privileges during the Mongol invasion; though they got them back from Béla IV 1243. The settlement joined to the Szent Anna quarter spreading after the Mongol invasion.

12. Szent Anna quarter recieved its name from the huge St. Anna's Church founded in 1272, and the friary of the Augustinian Order, which were situated at the big bend of the main road (now Bajcsi—Zsilinszky út) at the foot of Szent Tamás Hill. Beside the friary a college was established by Andrew III in 1290, which was functioning till the Turkish wars. The main owner of the quarter was the chapter. 14th—15th—century charters say that on the north—eastern side of the main road the ornamented stone houses of the canons were situated.

In the area between Szent Tamás Hill and the Little—Danube, where the waters of the thermal springs formed a lake (in the area of the present Fürdő Szálló — spa hotel — and swimming pool), developed

13. Héviz (thermal water) or Tapolca quarter. The stone houses of the canons erected here near the lake, mainly at the foot of the hill, around the public bath (balnea communia), which was built by the wife of Béla III, later bestowed on the Hospitallers in Szentkirály by Béla IV in 1238. The latter founded a hospice and a church in honour of St. Elizabeth beside the bath. The stone palace of the famous historiographer of King Luis the Great, János

THE RUINS OF ESZTERGOM AFTER THE SIEGE OF 1595 —
part of the etching by Georg Houfnagel

THE GATE OF THE ESZTERGOM CASTLE in 1820
(based on the drawing of Jaschke, by an unknown artsist)

Tótsolymosi Apród, the Archdeacon of Küküllő, stood near it in the vicinity of other buildings. On the outflow of Lake Héviz the water mill of the chapter worked already from the 13th century.

14. The church of the St. Thomas provostry was built either by King Béla III or Archbishop Jób in honour of St. Thomas á Becket martyred in 1170. Round the church on the top of the hill, the houses of six canons of the chapter were situated; on the eastern gentle slopes the settlement of the serfs and garderns and vineyards were to be found.

In the valley between St. Thomas Hill and Várhegy developed

15. Libád. St. Ambrose' Church mentioned first in a charter in 1331 must have been the parish church of this settlement, and Libád was the estate of the Esztergom chapter.

16. Petény quarter was situated north of the Várhegy on the Danube bank. The busy road through it led to the most important ferry of the area, the Kakat ferry (the name of the present town of Párkány was Kakat in the Árpádian age), which was already mentioned in a charter of Garamszentbenedek in 1075. There is data about stone houses of burghers besides the estates of the archbishop and the chapter on the settlement, which was the 'suburbium' of the castle, from the 14th—15th centuries. To the north of Petény lay

17. Szentgyörgymező (St. George's Field) around the provostry of St. George on the bank of the Danube. The provostry (the church of which stood in the place of the today's parish church) must have been founded already in the 12th century, though the first trustworthy mention is known in the 1230. First it had four then eight canons; its provost had the fifth place in the cathedral chapter, and was the archdeacon of the cathedral as well.

There is data about another church, the church of the Virgin Mary, in Szentgyörgymező. This may have been the parish church of the settlement. At the beginning of the 1980s the excavations over the built—up area of the present settlement opened up the remains of 10th—12th century houses. In the north of the royal town

18. on the Island beside the convent and church of the Benedictine nuns, founded probably in the 11th century, there was a smaller settlement as well.

The buildings devastated in the 16th—17th centuries were mostly excavated between 1980 and 1993. Beside the three—aisled church of the Árpádian age, the remains of the convent, in its yard those of a sepulchrial chapel and other interesting archaelogical finds came to light as well as some details of houses belonging to the settlement.

The quarters of the town, built closely together were introduced above. The settlement, Fenyérd (Fenerd) was built a little further among the hills. The others lying even further (Bylle, Bajon, Peszér, Úrkuta, Zamárd and Ákospalota) belonged to Esztergom, but were independent villages. The town of Esztergom was actually formed by the conglomerate of the above—mentioned 18 settlements. However, this significant medieval town was already seriously damaged in 1526; then during the wars of the 150—year Turkish rule it was almost completely destroyed; in its place a town of much less importance was built.

THE MEETING OF FREDERICK BARBAROSSA AND BÉLA III

On 11 May 1189 Frederick Barbarossa, Emperor of the Holy Roman Empire left Regensburg for the Holy Land to keep his promise concerning the crusade. He chose the road by land and on foot, unlike Philip Augustine, the French king and Richard Coeur—de—Lion, the king of England. This road used by the crusaders already for a long time led through Hungary, where King Béla III was the ruler at that time.

The meetings of kings is stricktly determined by the protocol, whether it is official talks or a private meeting; this is true about the Middle Ages as well. Barbarossa, as the sovereign of another country asked King Béla for the permission to cross his land well in advance. Chronicles report that the crusaders did not always behave as pious pilgrims were expected; even though it was well—known that pious pilgrims were not really gentle knights. Once King Coloman had to fight crusaders that plundered to over come the shortage of food. By Béla's time the conditions already changed; and Barbarossa tried to discipline his army, too. He reached the Hungarian border about 24 May, after he had to send back five hundred soldiers from Vienna — as his contemporary, the Benedictine abbey, Arnold Lübeck writes — 'from his rakish, stealing and other good-for-nothing people'. (This means the discipline was not so perfect when the army reached big towns like Vienna.) The Emperor celebrated Whitsun on the frontier on 29 May,

and continued his journey on 31. King Béla had aready been informed about his arrival, and — as Arnold writes — sent legates to welcome him and give him the King's permission to cross the country. He also 'promised that they are allowed to buy any goods to their liking'. This was not an easy procedure as the Germans had to change their money into Hungarian denarii, and the parties were not always satisfied. Another chronicle says:

'The Hungarians defrauded us only when exchanging denarii and silver, as for two denarii from Cologne they only gave five Hungarian denarii, for two from Friesach only four, for one from Regensburg or Krems only one, though a Hungarian denarius was hardly worth one from Verona.'

All this means that there must have been centrally determined exchange rates; and the King had a pretty income from the exchange of money, and besides he also helped the Hungarian money to spread.

The King tried to speed up the march of the crusaders across one of the richest parts of his country by improving the condition of the roads; it has to be mentioned, however, that no sovereign was happy to accept so many armed and hungry soldiers in his country.

'The King ordered that, as soon as they stepped on Hungarian land, bridges should be laid over rivers, brooks and marshes.' Thus the Germans were travelling relatively without difficulties as far as

Esztergom, where the meeting of the two sovereigns took place.

Béla III, who was brought up in Byzantium, learned the tricks of diplomacy very well; this was reflected in the opinions formed about him in other countries. According to Richard of London, a crusader—choricle writer

'The king of the Hungarians, called Béla, was delighted to meet the Emperor. This man was favoured by nature: his tall figure, noble face and his dignity entitle him to be a sovereign.' When the graves of Béla III and his first. wife, Ann of Antiochia were found in Székesfehérvár in the last century, antropological research aslo proved that the English chronicle writer had been right: King Béla was a tall, hawk—nosed, hard—featured, sovereign—looking man.

Béla received the Emperor personally outside the town of Esztergom, which was mentioned by the chronicle writer as 'the capital of the Hungarians'. This courtesy had practical reasons as well, as in spite of all the previous agreement and 'safety measures' the Hungarian king did not really believe that the German crusaders would cross the country quietly without any incidents. So he considered it important to have negotiations personally, which seemed to be successful. During the four—day stay of the Emperor — Abbey Arnold writes:

'On the advice of the noblemen the firm and lasting peace was also confirmed with oaths of the soldiers who were often unquiet and boistrerous.' Our King seems to have been 'both hospitable and compliant'.

The first husband of the King's wife, the French Margaret Capet was the 'younger English king', the son of Henry, the English king, who was crowned still in his father's life. He was a famous knight all over Europe (among others he started to patronize William Marshal, a knight—errant, who later rose to a very high position); so the knightly ideals and customs were well—known in the Hungarian court, among them the custom that the highborn guest was presented by the mistress of the house, which can often be read about in romances (Margaret's sister—in—law, Mary of Champagne, patronized Chrétien de Troyes, who wrote the most beautiful pieces of court epic, among them the legend of King Arthur). The chrolicle says:

'The Queen bestowed on the Emperor a splendid tent covered completely with scarlet carpets, a bed with a valuable blanket and pillows and an ivory chair with a cushion which stood in front of the bed. They were so artistically made that it cannot be expressed by this modest writing. And so as the Emperor does not miss any conceivable splendour, a tiny little white hunting dog was running to and fro on the carpet.' And again as in a romance, the Queen turned to the Emperor and asked him for something which no chivalrous sovereign was able to refuse, namely she asked him to intercede with King Béla for his brother, Prince Géza, who had been in captivity for fifteen years. At Barbarossa's request Béla released his brother; the chronicle does not mention though with what feelings, just suggests that he only obeyed the unwritten rule of hospitality. 'The King, who received the Emperor with great respect, did not want to sadden him, so at his request he not only released his brother but ordered him to prepare and show the road, riding with two thousand Hungarians before the Emperor.' This must have been another safety measure to protect partly the Emperor, partly the released Prince and partly the settlements on the way of the crusaders.

While the army was waiting on the other side of the River Garam, the King entertained Barbarossa in the more and more beautiful Esztergom castle.

The King also provided for the food supply of the army. He gave two store—houses of flour to the Emperor, who distributed it partly in his army, partly among the poor. As it often happened, a fight began and the chronicle says three people were buried by the flour.

Then the King took Barbarossa to Óbuda, which Arnold called 'Attila's town'. The Emperor hunted here for four days then followed his journey along the River Tisza, where he was accompanied by the Hungarian King. Barbarosa needed more food supply; and at the River Száva (Sava) after counting his soldiers, he arranged a tournament in honour of the Hungarian King and knighted sixty squires. It is not known whether they were Hungarians or Germans but that means we have early data about Hungarian tournaments; and even if this one was organized by the Emperor, the Hungarian sovereign must have participated in it. At the River Morave the King took leave from the Emperor, giving him rich presents as was usual: 'four camels(!) loaded with expensive presents in the value of five thousand marks.'

THE FUNERAL INSIGNIA OF KING BÉLA III

The finds from the only intact royal grave opened up in the last century are simple and bad—quality copies of the royal insignia. The originals must have been much more magnificent; the objects put in graves were only symbols. King Béla III was buried beside his first wife, Ann of Antiochia, who came from the Holy Land; this certainly influenced Béla's behaviour with the crusaders.

CONRAD III AND LUIS VII MARCH ACROSS HUNGARY WITH THEIR CRUSADERS

Miniature from the Illuminated Chronicle.

The route of almost all the crusades led across Hungary. The sovereign of the Holy Roman Empire and the French king marched across Hungary with the armies during the Second Crusade.

THE CHRONOLOGY OF ESZTERGOM

350 B.C.	Celtic settlement and oppidum
1th—4th B. C.	Roman settlement and castrum: Solva
	c. 970 Vajk (St. Stephen) born
972—997	Prince Géza's seat
1000—1256	Royal seat
1001—	Archbishopric see
1240—42 A	Winter Mongols destroy Esztergom but cannot occupy the castle
1270	King Béla IV buried here
1450—1470	The construction of 'Vitéz János' palace
1506	The construction of Bakócz's chapel
1543	Sultan Suleiman occupies Esztergom
1594	Siege to reoccupy the castle — poet Bálint Balassi dies
1595	The castle reoccupied
1605—1683	The Esztergom castle in the hands of the Turks — John Sobiesky, the Polish king reoccupies it
1706	Prince Ferenc Rákóczi occupies the whole castle

BIBLIOGRAPHY

Csorba, Csaba: Eszergom hadi krónikája (The Military Chronicle of Eszergom). Budapest 1978.
Csorba, Csaba: Eszergom (Panoráma: Magyar városok) Budapest 1981.
Dercsényi, Dezső—Zolnay, László: Eszergom (Magyar Müemlékek) Budapest 1956.
Horváth, István—Kelemen, Márta—Torma, István: Komárom megye régészeti topográfiája (Eszergom és a dorogi járás) (The Archaelogical Topography of Komárom County) in: Magyarország régészeti topográfiája. Budapest 1979.
Leopold, Antal: Szent István király születési helye (The Birthplace of King St. Stephen) in: Szent István Emlékkönyv II. Budapest 1938.
Némethy, Lajos: Emléklapok Eszergom múltjából (From the History of Eszergom). Eszergom 1900.
Horváth, István—Vukov, Konstantin: Vitéz János eszergomi palotája. (The Eszergom Palace of János Vitéz) Tata 1986.
Zolnay, László: A középkori Eszergom. (The Medieval Eszergom.) Budapest 1983.

THE OPENING HOURS OF THE MUSEUMS

Balassa Bálint Múzeum
2501 Esztergom, Pázmány P. u. 13.
Open: 9 am—5 pm , closed on Monday

Keresztény Múzeum (Ecclesiastical Museum)
2500 Esztergom, Mindszenty tér 2.
Open: 10 am—5 pm , closed on Monday

Vármúzeum (Castle Museum)
2500 Esztergom, Szt. István tér 1.
Open: 9 am—5 pm , closed on Monday

Bazilika—Kincstár (Basilica—Treasury)
2500 Esztergom, Szent István tér 2.
Open: 10 am—4 pm

Duna Múzeum (Museum of Hydrology)
2500 Esztergom, Kölcsey u. 2.
Open: 9 am—5 pm , closed on Monday

Babits Mihály Emlékmúzeum (Mihály Babits' House)
2500 Esztergom, Babits Mihály út 11.
Open: 10 am—5 pm from May to October, closed on Monday

SZÉKESFEHÉRVÁR

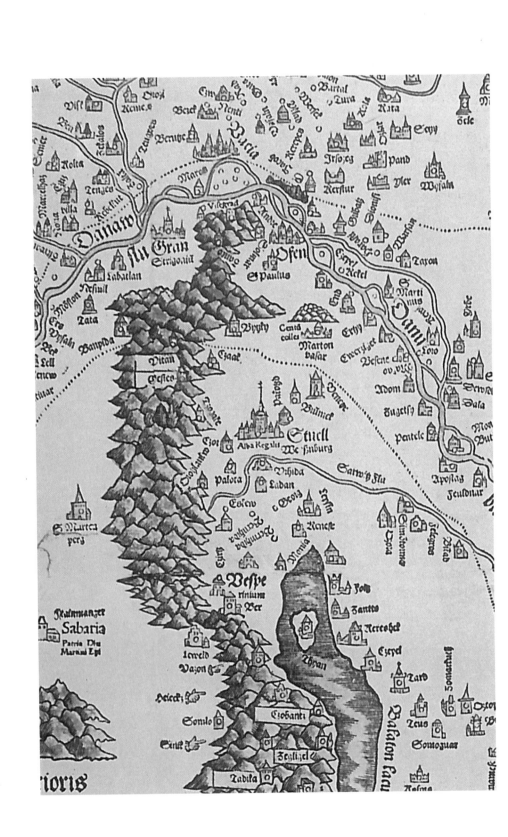

SZÉKESFEHÉRVÁR

One of the most important towns of the medieval Hungary was situated on the dry area protected by the marshland where the Bakony Hills meet Mezőföld. People found a living place on this pebbly stretch of land already in the neolithic age. In the copper age and bronze age a densely populated conglomerate of settlements was to be found here, in the place of the later coronation town. Celtic tribes settled here, too; and pottery from the Roman times proves that people lived here in this period as well.

According to Master Simon Kézai after the Hungarians conquered Pannonia, Árpád pitched his tent where later the town of Székesfehérvár was built. Kézai says that 'this place was the first dwelling place of Chieftain Árpád'.

The author of the Illuminated Chronicle, Mark Kálti writes that as Chieftain Árpád had pitched his camp on Noah Hill near Székesfehérvár, 'King St. Stephen, who was his descendent, founded the town of Székesfehérvár in the vicinity'.

It is, however, very possible that there was a princely house and a church in Székesfehérvár already in the time of Prince Géza, as later sources say Géza and his wife Adelheid were buried in St. Peter's Church here. The princely centre developed into a royal residence playing an important role already during the reign of King Stephen. It was surrounded with walls in the first half of the 11th century. Prince St. Emeric was born in the palace here in 1007.

The early castle had a square plan, in the middle of which was a church of quatrefoil plan, which was founded in honour of St. Peter. In 1225 Béla IV rebuilt the church, two towers on the eastern side suggest an earlier reconstruction period as well. Béla was crowned in this church in 1235. In this period the building complex of the royal palace was erected along the squared-planned ramparts which were enlarged with a semicircular terrace in the south.

To the north-east of the early royal castle were the building complex of the provostry and the basilica with curtain walls around them. King St. Stephen founded the royal basilica in honour of the Blessed Virgin Mary, which was standing in the axis of the building complex. Its size can be characeried by the number of its altars and side chapels — in the age of the House of Árpád there were five, but in later periods this number can be estimated at thirty-forty.

The garth and the cloister were situated to the south of the basilica, the rooms of the chapter and chapels opened from here. St. Antony's hostelry mentioned in 1370 and the school of the provostry founded by St. Stephen must have stood here.

The palace of the provost, mentioned only in the 15th century, stood in the north side of the royal basilica. Archaelogical finds prove that there were settlements both on the north and the south sides of the ecclesiastical centre surrounded by ramparts, lying in the axis of the later city.

Their number has not been decided, but it is certain that their buildings except for the churches were not made of durable materials. The traces of the buildings made of timber and isolated with mud and daub remained in the post-holes found during the excavations. The market place (Theatrum Civitas), which was first mentioned in a charter in 1433, was situated in the north side of the early royal castle. On the north side of this was the settlement and church of the merchants. To the east was St. Bartholomew's parish Church and the cemetery of the serfs of the king in the centre of the above-mentioned settlement. The settlement of the serfs of the chapter, their parish church consecrated to the Holy Cross and their cemetery were north of the building complex of the provostry. Though it already was typical of the Árpádian age, in the 13th—14th centuries the medieval Székesfehérvár was surrounded by a whole conglomeration of settlements.

In the Middle Ages Székesfehérvár was the scene of the sessions of the parliament, coronations, funerals, royal weddings, christenings and often also that of fights for the throne. The army of Emperor Henry III seated the expelled Peter Orseolo on the throne in 1044. Later the troops of the pagan Vata entered Székesfehérvár with Princes Andrew and Levente without any fights. In 1051 Henry III besieged the town again. The settlements below the secular and ecclesiastical centres, i.e. the town, were already considered the capital of the country; as — the German Altaich Yearbook proves — Prince Solomon called Emperor Henry IV 'to Székesfehérvár, the metropolis of the country'. Géza and St. Ladislas marched with their armies into Székesfehérvár after the Mogyoród battle (1074); and while the crusaders were going across the country, there were also fights in the town.

The privileges of the burghers of the town, which was famous for its markets and played an important role in the division of salt, were perhaps given by St. Stephen and confirmed by Béla IV.

The fortified Székesfehérvár castle protected also by marshland withstood the sieges of the Mongols. In spite of this, referring to safety, King Béla IV settled the Latin burghers of the town in the early royal castle and palace. In the place of the monastery of the provostry the street of the canons was built, the early villages disappear, and around the churches, stone houses were built along a new network of streets, which was the same as today.

The ramparts enclosing the inner town and in its north-eastern corner the new royal castle and palace were built by the end of the 13th century. To the north of the inner town lay the Budai suburb (Civitas Exterior), its collegiate church, St. Nicholas was mentioned in 1215. Its earthworks and ditches may have been built in the 15th—16th centuries. The parish church in honour of St. Dominic was mentioned in a charter in 1331, the Virgin Mary convent of the Dominican nuns in 1276, the Franciscan friary in 1260, St. Elizabeth's parish Church in 1437 and the chapel consecrated to the Virgin Mary in 1543.

The dry area to the west of the inner town was protected by mounds and hedges. Újváros (new town) (Nova Civitas) (1327) was situated in the north; it had several ecclesiastical institutions: Archangel St. Michael's Church and friary of the Augustianians (1303), the friary and St. Margaret's Church of the Dominicans (1221), St. Mark's friary (1372) and several stone buildings. On the south-western part of the dry area was the monastery and other buildings of the Hospitallers of St. John of Jerusalem, founded by Archbishop Martirius of Esztergom.

The village of Szentkirályfölde belonging to the Hospitallers was situated on a peninsula, south of the friary possibly already in the first half of the 12th century. Its parish church first mentioned in a charter in 1192 was consecrated to St. Stephen. Data from 1272 says Queen Eufrosina was buried here.

The estate of the chapter, the village of Ingovány (swamp), mentioned first in 1372 was also situated on the dry area but south of the inner town. Its parish church was consecrated to St. Cosma and Damian — as a charter from 1537 says.

To the south of Ingovány, on the south dry area Újfalu (Nova Villa) was situated, it was mentioned in 1298. Its parish church may have been St. Martin's Church standing there already in 1096.

THE MEDIEVAL REMAINS OF THE HOSPITALLERS' MONASTERY

THE REMAINS OF THE NORTH-EASTERN BASTION *built around 1473* AND ITALIAN BASTION *built around 1601—1602*

WHITE MARBLE PARAPET WITH TWINING *from the early royal palace, 11th c.*

WHITE MARBLE FONT WITH HEADS *from the monastery of the Hospitallers, 12th c.*

MEDALLION WITH EAGLE, *lead and glass, from the 12th—c. early royal castle*

THE 'DREIHAUSEN' GOBLET, CRAKOW-SHAPED, ORNAMENTED WITH A WOMAN'S HEAD, *German stoneware from the moanstery of the Hospitallers, mid-15th c.*

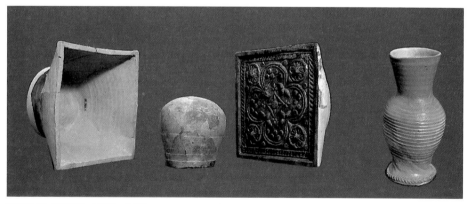

STOVE TILES AND CUP, *stoneware from a canon's house excavared in front of St. Ann's Chapel*

LEATHER SHOE, *Heimer house, 15th c.*

ST. ANN'S CHAPEL,
the end of the 15th c.

BRONZE CANDLESTICK,
Heimer house, 15th c.

HENRY IV AND HIS ARMY ACCOMPANY KING SOLOMON TO SZÉKESFEHÉRVÁR

Initial, Illuminated Chronicle (14th c) In the left of the picture, the drawing of the royal basilica with four towers and buttresses can be seen.

King Béla I died in 1063. His oldest son, Géza, wanted to ascend the throne. King Andrew's expelled son, Solomon asked his brother-in-law, Emperor Henry IV for military help to be able to ascend the throne. The troops of Henry IV marched into the capital of the country, Székesfehérvár ('ad Wizinburg, que est regni sui metropolis'), where Solomon was received 'with great respect by the whole clergy and people of Hungary'. Solomon was crowned in the royal basilica, and he came to the throne. Solomon's mother presented Henry IV with a sword (Attila's sword) which is now in the Schatzkammer in Vienna.

ST. LADISLAS — *Hungarian Angevin Legendary (c 1337)*
1. St. Ladislas marches in Székesfehérvár; 2. St. Ladislas is crowned.
After they destroyed King Solomon's army in the Mogyoród battle (14 March 1074), St. Ladislas and his brother Géza went with their escort to Székesfehérvár, which they fortified with selected soldiers. As the Illuminated Chronicle writes, Géza — 'urged by the Hungarians' — was crowned in the royal basilica, but he died soon, in April 1077. After his death St. Ladislas was crowned also in Székesfehérvár, though earlier he had always avoided political power.

After the death of King Matthias, Wladislas II (Jagello) was the Hungarian king, he was crowned in Székesfehérvár. Shortly after this, however, Maximilian Hapsburg, Roman king, referring to the 1463 Sopron treaty, was pretender to the Hungarian throne, and marched to Hungary with his troops. Maximilian approached Székesfehérvár on 9 November 1490, one of the suburbs of which was put on fire by the defenders. The German troops occupied the Budai suburb and the city amid cruel destruction. The mercenaries ransacked the royal basilica and its treasures and the graves of the kings. ⟫➜

HANS SPRINGINKLEE: THE TROOPS OF MAXIMILIAN I BESIEGE SZÉKESFEHÉRVÁR IN 1490, *wood engraving (the beginning of the 16th c)*

WILHELM DILLICH: THE VIEW OF SZÉKESFEHÉRVÁR FROM THE NORTH-WEST
C 1593, wood engraving, Kassel (1600)
Dillich depicts the inner town encirled with walls, the Budai suburb to the north and Újfalu to the south. To the north-west of the inner town, behind the Sziget (island) or Palotai Gate protected with round bastions, the suburb earlier called Nova Civitas can be seen, which was then called Sziget quarter.

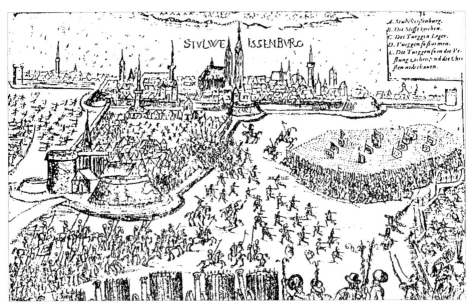

W. P. ZIMMERMANN: TURKS IN FRONT OF SZÉKESFEHÉRVÁR IN 1602, AT THE TIME OF THE REOCCUPATION *(the beginning of the 17th c)*
The etching depicts Sziget quarter (Nova Civitas) with its barbican, the inner town, Budai suburb and Nova Villa. Near the gate, researchers dealing with the history of the later Rácváros (Serbian town) identified a 'Serbian' church.

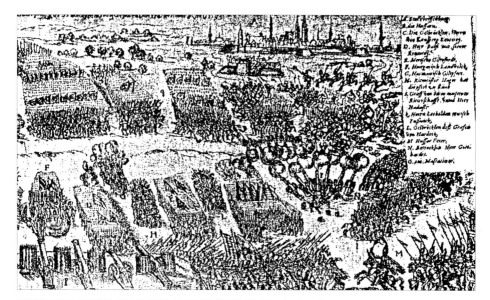

WILHELM PETER ZIMMERMANN'S ETCHING: *the battle in 1593*

WILHELM PETER ZIMMERMANN'S ETCHING: *the 13 October situation of the battle (the beginning of the 17th c)*

Zimmermann depicts the west side of the inner town from the north-western round bastion to the southern round bastion; in the north Budai quarter, in the south Nova Villa can be seen. The etching also shows 16th—17th c. weapons and battle equipment. To the north-west — as in Dillich's etching — the barbican of Nova Civitas can be seen.

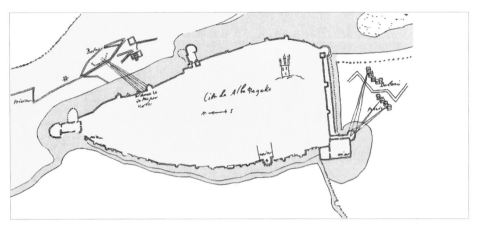

PLAN WITH ITALIAN INSCRIPTION: *'Citta de Alba Regalle' (Karlsruhe, Landesarchiv 1601)*

This is the first plan of Székesfehérvár, trustworthy in the details but inaccurate in size. In the centre the inner town can be seen, its fortifications are described even in minor details. Besides them the representation of the royal basilica is of outstanding interest, its chancel is in the ramparts. In the north-eastern corner the newer royal castle can be seen beside the Budai Gate. Three suburbs and their fortifications are on the plan in the northern, southern and western sides of the inner town.

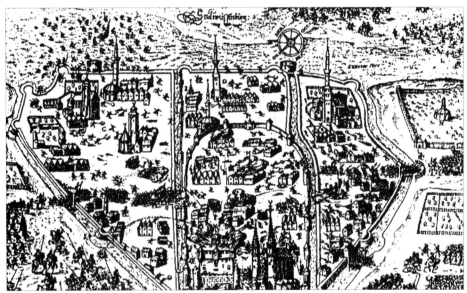

W. PETER ZIMMERMANN'S ETCHING: THE SIEGE OF SZÉKESFEHÉRVÁR IN 1601 *(the beginning of the 17th c.)*

It shows the inner town and the three quarters of Székesfehérvár; moreover, the newer royal castle and palace, the royal basilica and some known churches. It is obvious, though, that the artist did not see the town, worked only after narrations.

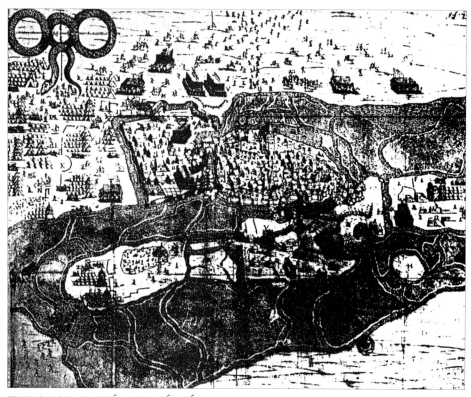

THE SIEGE OF SZÉKESFEHÉRVÁR.
The so-called French engraving shows the 1601 siege. It depicts the inner town, suburbs, fortifications, churches, the newer royal castle and palace. The villages represented in the etching have been found during the field-work.

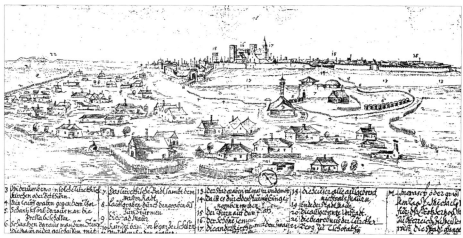

SZÉKESFEHÉRVÁR AFTER THE SIEGE IN 1601. (*German sketch, 1601. Karlsruhe,
Landesarchiv*)

It shows the western part of the medieval Székesfehérvár. In the foreground Sziget suburb and its fortifications and hedges depicted in the Italian plan can be seen, near the Palotai Gate of the inner town the tower of a church, the remains of the royal basilica and the nave and double towers of St. Peter's Church.

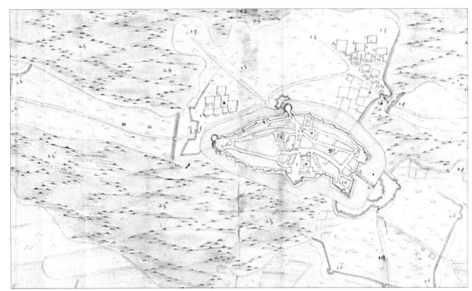

LA VERGNE'S SURVEY SHEET ABOUT SZÉKESFEHÉRVÁR *(Vienna, Kriegsarchiv, 1689)*
This is the first trustworthy plan of Székesfehérvár. From the medieval buildings, the detailed representation of the ramparts in the inner town are worth mentioning with the buildings of the Turkish times, the remains of St. Peter's Church, the present St. Ann's Chapel, the royal basilica and the palace of the provost as well as the marked ruins of the newer royal castle and palace beside them. This plan shows first the street system of the medieval town. La Vergne depicted the destroyed remains of Budai quarter and Nova Villa as well as the village of Ingovány and Sziget quarter.

SZÉKESFEHÉRVÁR FROM THE EAST (F. B. Werner's etching, c 1741)
It last represented the eastern side of the ramparts of the medieval Székesfehérvár in intact condition. Among the Baroque buildings appearing already, the Gothic chancel between the two towers of St. Peter's Church and St. Ann's Chapel of medieval origin are worth mentioning.

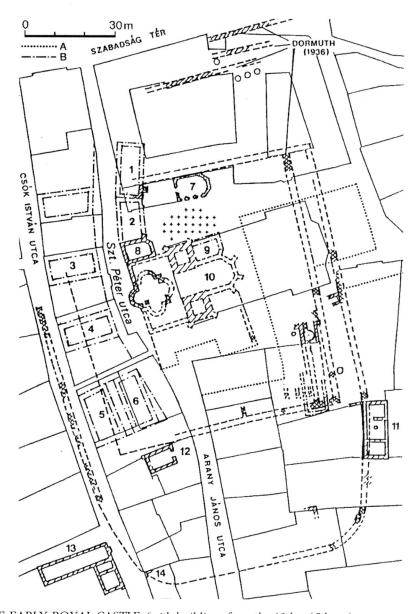

THE EARLY ROYAL CASTLE *(with buildings from the 13th—15th cc.)*

1—6. Medieval sites and remains of houses
7   St. Anna's Chapel
8   The chapel of a burgher, Hentel
9   Sacristy
10   St. Peter's Church (in various
       construction periods)

11   9 Kossuth utca: a medieval house
12   Medieval cellar
13   17 Megyeház utca: a medieval house
A — the borders of medieval sites
B — reconstructed medieval houses

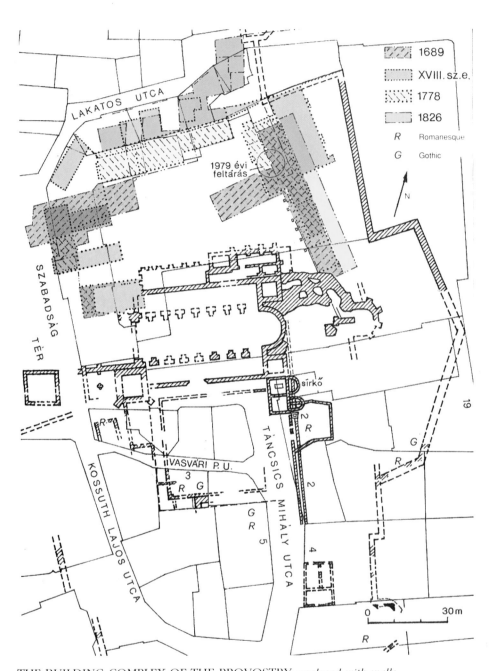

THE BUILDING COMPLEX OF THE PROVOSTRY *enclosed with walls*

The royal basilica was in the axis of the building complex developed in several construction periods, the palace of the provost and the buildings belonging to it can be placed to the north on the evidence of the excavations in 1797 and old town plans. The cloister and the rooms opening from here, belonging to the friary of the provost were situated south of the basilica.

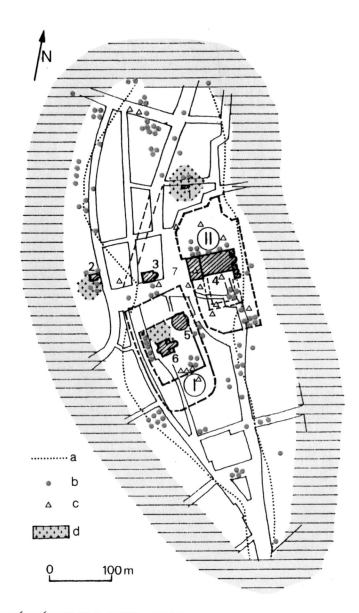

SZÉKESFEHÉRVÁR IN THE 11TH—13TH cc.
a = height above the level of the Adriatic Sea (110 m)
b = Árpádian sites and finds
c = the site where Romanesque stone carvings were found
d = medieval cemetery
I. Early royal castle and palace, II. the building complex of the provostry, 1. the church of the Holy Cross, 2. St. Bartholomew's Church, 3. the church of the settlement of merchants, 4. the royal basilica, 5. the supposed place of St. Emeric's Church, 6. St. Peter's Church, 7. Theatrum Civitatis

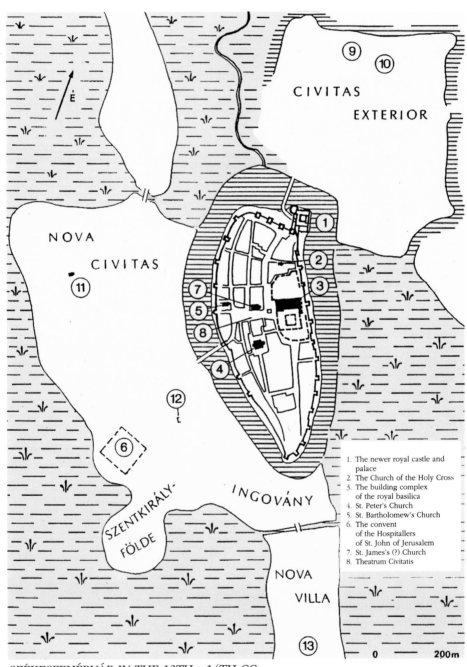

CIVITAS EXTERIOR

NOVA CIVITAS

NOVA VILLA

INGOVÁNY

SZENTKIRÁLY-FÖLDE

1. The newer royal castle and palace
2. The Church of the Holy Cross
3. The building complex of the royal basilica
4. St. Peter's Church
5. St. Bartholomew's Church
6. The convent of the Hospitallers of St. John of Jerusalem
7. St. James's (?) Church
8. Theatrum Civitatis

0   200m

SZÉKESFEHÉRVÁR IN THE 13TH—14TH CC.

The town already had ramparts, the newer royal castle and palace and newly developed street system and suburbs.

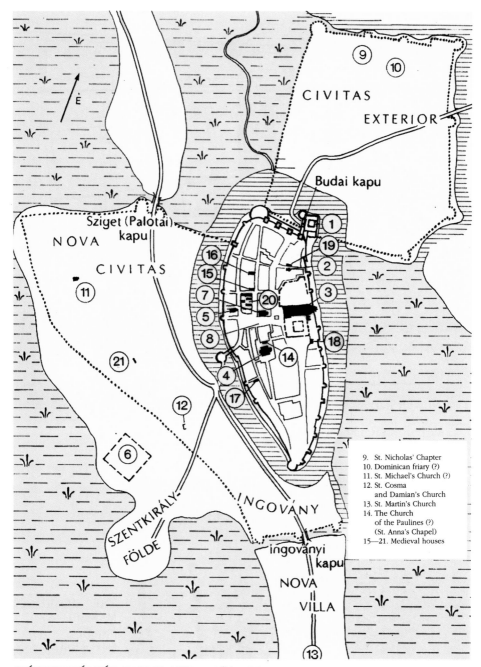

9. St. Nicholas' Chapter
10. Dominican friary (?)
11. St. Michael's Church (?)
12. St. Cosma
    and Damian's Church
13. St. Martin's Church
14. The Church
    of the Paulines (?)
    (St. Anna's Chapel)
15—21. Medieval houses

SZÉKESFEHÉRVÁR IN THE 15TH—16TH CC.
The plan shows the developed and modernized 14th—c. town with already fortified suburbs.

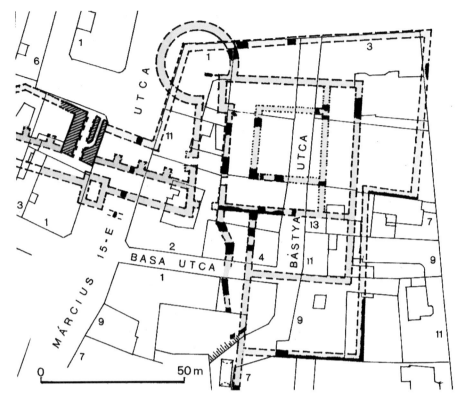

THE NEWER ROYAL CASTLE, reconstruction based on Árpád Dormuth's excavations

◼ the turn of the 13th—14th centuries   ▨ 16th century

☐ 1601—1602   ▨ 1647

THE TOMB OF MAXIMILIAN I, *detail* Maximilian occupies Székesfehérvár on 19 November 1490 (The imperial court church, Hofkirche, Innsbruck)

THE CHURCH
OF ST. MARY'S PROVOSTRY
IN SZÉKESFEHÉRVÁR
(THE ROYAL BASILICA)

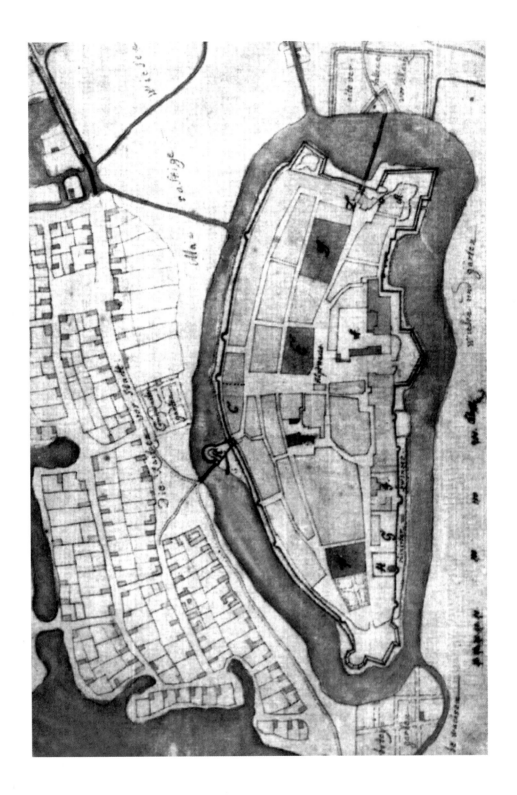

King Stephen, who after his corona-
tons at the beginning of 1001, who
joined his country to the Christian
West and who was canonized in
1083, founded and built his church,
which he chose as his burial-place as
well, beside the Jerusalem road — so
important for the Christian West — in
Székesfehérvár. The church — as legends from the time of the canonization have it — was consecrated to St.
Mary. It was mentioned on the
inscription of the chasuble used later
as coronation robe, which was
bestowed on St. Mary's Church in
Székesfehérvár by King Stephen and
his wife Gisele: ECCLESIAE SANCTAE
MARIAE SITAE IN CIVITATE ALBA.
The clergymen of the church formed
the provostry of St. Mary, the members
of which performed the duties of the
royal church. Sources say that Prince
Emeric, who died young on 1031,
was buried first in St. Mary's Church.
In 1038, when Stephen died, the
building was not consecrated yet, i.e.
it was not accomplished yet; as the
St. Stephen legend written by Bishop
Hartvik says: '... after conferring the
prelates decided to consecrate the
basilica first and only after it should
the body be buried'. Stephen and
Emeric's graves were not side by side
as the story in the legend about St.
Emeric says: a German man, Konrad,
who hoped absolution from his
heinous sins, after visiting the graves
of several saints at the end of his pilgrimage arrived at St. Stephen's grave,
where he fell asleep. St. Stephen
appeared in his dream, saying '... I am
not enough to intercede for you. Go
to my son, St. Emeric's grave, he
should be your intermediary'. After he
woke up, Konrad hurried 'to St.

Emeric's grave, which was in the same
church', and magic signs proved he
had been given absolution.
According to Hartvik, St. Stephen was
buried in the middle of the church.
The place rightful for the founder of
the church meant the axis of the
nave. According to this Alán
Kralovánszky excavated and identified the remains of a grave cased carefully with ashlers with St. Stephen's
grave.

St. Mary's Church as the church of
the sovereign had a wider range of
duties than just the accomplishement
of ecclesiastical tasks. The throne
stood here, most probably since this
part of the building was ready;
though its place in the church was
only mentioned in Pope Alexander
III's letter to Béla III in 1179.

The tradition to guard the regalia —
among them the most important, the
crown — is also considered to date in
Stephen's time. A Byzantine source
speaks about this first in 1166, mentioning the capital of Hungary with
the coronation church and the crown
of the Hungarian sovereigns kept
there.

The facts that the church was
founded by Stephen, whose grave
was there, too, and also that it had
special duties, made the church greatly important; several coronation and
wedding ceremonies were held here.
Concerning coronation the significance of the building can obviously
perceived in the contemporary
sources about struggles for the throne
after St. Stephen's death. After he
defeated Samuel Aba in Ménfő (1044),
Emperor Henry III marched to
Székesfehérvár with his army. '... They
were received with royal pomp, and

the Emperor invested Peter with the royal regalia, and he led Peter to the throne himself.' The historical data helped to create the tradition which only considered the coronation in Székesfehérvár legal. Only some elements of the coronation ceremony can be found in sources about the age of the House of Árpád and the 14th century; detailed description only remained from the 15th century .

We know the steps of the coronation of the child Ladislas in 1440 from Mrs Helena Kottanner's memoirs and the description of the coronation of Wladislas II from Bonfini. The elements of the coronation ceremony took place in different parts of the town: the jurisdiction in St. Peter's Church, the secular oath outdoors, the four sword-strokes towards the four cardinal points on the hill outside the town and the most significant events in the church. The most important details were: the oath of the king, the anointment of the king, putting on the coronation robe believed to have belonged to St. Stephen and girding the sword with the sword. Then the actual coronation followed when the Archbishop of Esztergom and the noblemen put the crown on the king's head, gave him the royal regalia — the scepre and the orb, and finally seated him on the throne. The Te Deum was sung and then the coronation mass closed the ceremony in the church. The last king crowned in Székesfehérvár was Ferdinand I on 3 November 1527.

The royal funerals started in the Székesfehérvár church after Stephen and Emeric were canonized in 1083.

After St. Stephen Coloman was the first king buried in St. Mary's Church.

Then out of nine Hungarian kings six were buried in this church in the 12th century: Coloman (+1116), Béla II (+1141), Géza II (+1162), Ladislas II, (+1163), Stephen IV (+1165), Béla III (+1196). The last king of the House of Árpád, the child King Ladislas III (+1205). In the 14th century after the House of Árpád died out, the new dynasty, the House of Anjou not only chose the Székesfehérvár church as their burial place but also developed the building. According to Thuróczy's chronicle Charles Robert's grave was beside the high altar, his son Luis the Great was buried in the chapel built by the king at the side of St. Mary's Church. In 1439 Albert Hapsburg was buried there, then in 1490 Matthias Hunyadi. King Matthias had significant construction work performed in the church, his tomb — as Tubero writes — was made of Transylvanian marble. St. Mary's Church was the burial place of the Hungarian kings till Székesfehérvár was occupied by the Turks in 1543. Wladislas II was buried here in 1516. The body of his son Luis II, who died in the Mohács battle, was brought here by John of Szapolyai in November 1526; it was put into a marble tomb — as György Szerémi writes — between the graves of Wladislas II and St. Emeric. The body of the last Hungarian king, John of Szapolya, who died in 1540 and was buried in the Székesfehérvár church, was removed by the Turks, so his final resting place is in St. Michael's Church.

The devastation of the building started during the Turkish occupation. Evlia Celebi writes that for some time the Christians were allowed to have church services there but then it was used for storing gunpower. During the 1601 siege of the town, when the Christians reoccupied Székesfehérvár for a year, its tower was blown up, thus the fate of the royal church was sealed. Its stones were used in the defence system of the town. In the 17th century Pecevi, Turkish historiographer writes about the building: '... in the middle of the castle there was a very tall magnificent church with a big domed building on its southern side, where already ten kings rested'.

THE REMAINS OF ST. MARY'S CHURCH, *the beginning of the 1940s*
The size and the main features of the church had been known since Imre Henszlmann's excavations in the last century; the ruins, however, were buried in the garden of the

palace of the bishop. For the 900th anniversary of St. Stephen's death one part of the garden was opened to the public to show the ruins after the excavation between 1936 and 1938. The remains of the walls were shown the visitors in their original condition without any completion. To east of it on the remains of the Monostorbástya an arcaded museum of stone carvings and the St. Stephen's mausoleum were erected according to the plans of Géza Lux. The 11th-century sarcophagus found in the 18th century was placed in the latter.

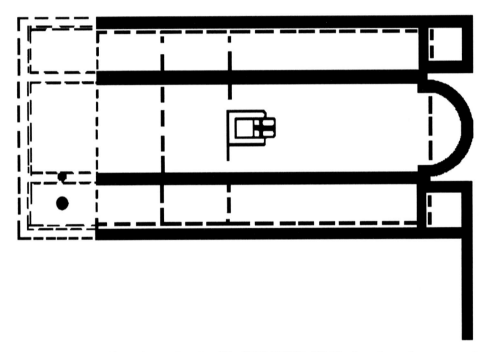

THE PLAN OF THE CHURCH IN ST. STEPHEN'S TIME, *based on the excaveted remains (recontruction by Alán Kralovánszy)*
The oldest part of the building was the 64 m long, 37.5 m wide, three-aisled basilica. It had a flat ceiling or an open-timbered roof. Its columns or pillars may have been joined with an arcade. During the excavations only the groundwalls of the columns or pillars were found, so the plan only shows this. Its main features were: a wide, semicircular chancel and square rooms in the corners of the building. The eastern rooms most probably served liturgy (sacristy, room for relics), but they certainly had functions in the coronation, guarding the crown, handling charters as well. The east-western directed, 10 m long band of the western rooms was a separate unit within the building; the rooms here were used in liturgy as well as the official duties of the king.

TOMB CALLED ST. STEPHEN'S SARCOPHAGUS, *11th century.*
The stone tomb called St. Stephen's sarcophagus since Elemér Varjú's study was published in 1930, which was carved from a Roman sarcophagus, is now considered to have been made around the canonization of St. Stephen for the relics found in the grave. Its ornamentation has partly kept the proportions of the Roman sarcophagus and partly refers to the Saint: at the end of the sarcophagus an angel is taking the soul of the deceased depicted as an infant to heaven.

THE VESTIBULE OF THE ÁRPÁDIAN CHURCH
The 13 m long vestibule joining to the church in the west, was built still in an early but still Roman period. Today above most of it the bishop's palace is situated. The part uncovered in the line of the southern aisle was an open vestibule, the arcades of which were walled up in the Árpádian period.

CAPITAL *from the the 12th c. church*
Because of the royal funerals the church was reconstructed and embellished after King Stephen and Prince Emeric were canonized. The building units were replaced with big pillars, the fragments of four of them with carefully carved Attic base can still be seen surrounded with the remains of the parts rebuilt later. Fragments of capitals from this period have been found partly near the church, partly in buildings in other areas of the town, built already in the modern times. The 95 cm tall carving in the picture is from the garden of the bishop's palace; near the acanthus leaves the fragments of an eagle snatching a rabbit can be seen.

CROWN FROM THE GRAVE OF KING BÉLA III.
The graves of Béla III and his wife, Ann of Antiochia were found intact in the area of St. Mary's Church. The graves came to light in a rescue excavation when a well was being bored in December 1848; and the finds were taken to the Hungarian National Museum. The coffins were made of red limestone panels held with iron clamps. In the King's grave there were a silver funeral crown and sceptre, a small sword also made for the funeral, a procession cross, a bracelet, a gold ring, enamelled jewellery and a pair of spurs; in the Queen's a similar crown, a gold ring and some fragments of textile woven with gold.

GOLD FILIGREE JEWELLERY FROM ROYAL GRAVES

In 1839 during drainage graves were stirred up in the area of the church. The gold jewellery found here, partly changed later, was taken to the National Museum. Among the finds there are studs of a belt , a tiny crown and a disc with Byzantine cloisonné enamel. The objects from the last third of the 12th century were made by the same goldsmiths who also prepared the filigree ornamentation of the coronation sceptre. In view of their age they may have originated from the grave of Ladislas III, who died in young age.

THE REMAINS OF THE PILLARS SEPARATING THE NAVE FROM THE SOUTH AISLE

The remains of the pillars witnessed large-scale reconstruction in the Middle Ages. The walls built to the eastern and western sides of the 12th-c. pillars were constructed in the age of Charles Robert. As the Thuróczy chronicle writes: '... the King started to cover St. Mary's Church in Székesfehérvár, which was often destroyed in blazes, with lead plates, to embellish with wonderful vaulting and to fortify with firm columns.'

FRAGMENTS OF CARVINGS FROM THE ANGEVIN SEPULCHRAL CHAPEL.

Our chronicles often mentioned the sepulchral chapel built by King Luis the Great, which — according to Bonfini — was a chapel of St. Stephen's basilica. It is difficult to decide where it was as there are very few remains of walls. The style of several fragments found in different parts of the town, however, prove that they undoubtedly belonged to the Angevin sepulchral chapel and the tomb there. The two red marble carvings though very fragmentedly but clearly show the figure of a king depicted with the sceptre and orb, so they certainly belonged to the tomb of King Luis the Great. When Charles the Small was crowned in 1385, the widowed Queen Elizabeth and her daughter, Mary — as Thuróczy says — 'bathed the red stone in tears when they saw the statue of the good king'. The relief with the ostrich crest of the House of Anjou must have decorated the wall of the sepulchral chapel.

THE REMAINS OF THE SOUTH-WESTERN TOWER.

A charter from 1425 says that Pipo Ozorai, a confidant of King Sigismund rebuilt the crumbling tower of the church, and under it he built a sepulchral chapel for himself and his wife, which was consecrated to Apostoles Philip and James and King St. Ladislas, the 'patron of Hungary'. The remains of the Gothic tower excavated in the south-western corner of the church can be identified with the tower of Pipo Ozorai; the scattered stones prove that it was blown up in 1601.

THE FOUNDATION WALL OF THE CHANCEL ENLARGED IN THE MATTHIAS PERIOD

The construction during the reign of Matthias changed the size and proportions of the church. It was lengthened with about 36m towards the east; the nave was re-vaulted; thus the church was converted into a huge Gothic building. Only parts of the foundation walls have remained from this period, which do not show much of the upper parts. Bonfini writes about the construction: 'A very tall vault was put up of ashlers, it began to rise at the apsis with so many sections of vaults that it surpassed even the most daring ideas. As it was built on marshland, its foundation was very deep.'

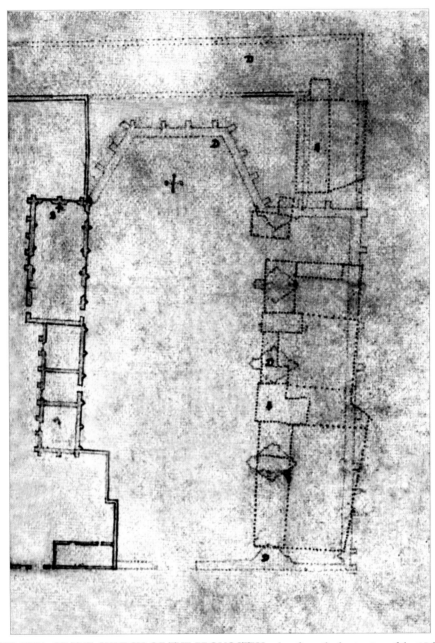

THE AREA OF THE CHURCH OF THE PROVOSTRY, *plan from the beginning of the 18th c.*
Sources after the liberation from the Turks at the end of the 17th and at the beginning of the
18th centuries only speak about two chapels in the place of the former royal church. When the
rebuilding started, Provost Barnabeis had his chapel here, and the German inhabitants also
used one of the chapels. The etching made in the 18th c. shows chapels and only the outline
of the church.

CORONATION
IN SZÉKESFEHÉRVÁR

In 1440 Whitsun was on 15 May.
Before it there had been a several-day
preparation in the old coronation
town of Székesfehérvár: a king was to
be crowned in the basilica. It was of
no importance that the would-be sovereign was a twelve-week-old infant
and that his mother, the daughter of
Emperor and King Sigismund, the
wife of King Albert took the possession of the crown in a not quite hon-
est way: she had it stolen with the
help of one of her ladies-in-waiting
from the Visegrád castle, where it was
guarded.

The way kings were crowned was
full of traditions all over Europe. The
act of anointment spread during the
Carolingians, it was the symbol of the
holiness of the king. The priest gave
the blessing of God's power to the
future king with the consecrated oil
thus entrusting him with prelate's
power as well. Later this ritual disappeared, but its can be discovered in a
belief in connection with the French
kings that an anointed sovereign is
able to cure by imposition of hands.

Even in the 18th century several
paralysed and invalid people went on
pilgrimage to Reims to be touched by
the king.

Concerning the coronation of the
Hungarian kings in the early period
we have no exact data; from about
1440, however, we have an extraordi-
nary source: the lady-in-waiting of
Queen Elizabeth, who actively participated in stealing the crown, Mrs
Helena Kottanner gives a detailed and
exciting description of the theft (in
February 1440), the flight and the
events in Székesfehérvár. She confirms
that there were traditions in the coronation ceremony, and because of
them Charles Robert was crowned
three times:

'Because there are three laws in the
Hungarian Kingdom, and he who
does not obey all of them is not considered the legal king. The first law is
that the Hungarian king has to be
crowned with the Holy Crown. The
second is that he has to be crowned
by the Archbishop of Esztergom. The
third says that the coronation has to
take place in Székesfehérvár.'

On the eve of Whitsun, after she
arrived in Székesfehérvár with her baby
son and small escort, the widowed
Queen summoned the old patricians of
the town, who still remebered the
coronation of her father, Sigismund in
1387; and agreed with them and her
loyal men on the details of the following day's ceremony. She showed then
the Holy Crown to prove that her son's
claim was legitimate.

Mrs Kottanner, who was the nurse
of Prince Ladislas, writes the following: 'I got up early, bathed the noble
King' (who did not yet have the title,
but as Mrs Kottanner wrote her memoirs later, she consequently called
him king) 'and I prepared him to the
best of my knowledge. Then he was
taken to the church where every king
is crowned.'

Earlier Mrs Kottanner writes about
how she sewed a suit of golden cloth
like the one kings wore at their coronation ceremony, the traditional robe
was certainly not suitable for a three-
month-old infant. Here she also
relates about a custom which was not
mentioned elsewhere: when they

arrived in the church, the roodscreen was closed and the burghers inside did not let Elizabeth in until she took an oath on something that the lady-in-waiting does not write about , but it is obvious from the events that the Queen had to confirm the privileges of the burghers of Székesfehérvár on behalf of her son. According to Mrs Kottanner Elizabeth spoke Hungarian, then everybody waiting outside was allowed in. The Queen had a daughter as well, the little four-year-old Princess Elizabeth, who was watching the ceremony from the organ loft as her mother did not want her to be in the crowd.

In the course of the mass the small prince was first confirmed, then knighted by Voivode Miklós Újlaki with the sword of Ulrik Cillei, which had the inscription: 'Unfalteringly'. During the knighting Ladislas was in the arm of Mrs Kottanner, who says Újlaki happened to hit the child with the sword a bit too strongly. 'The noble Queen standing beside me noticed this and said: For God's sake, you must not hurt him. He ensured her laughingly that the small prince would not be harmed.

Then Most Reverend Prelate, the Archbishop of Esztergom took the consecrated oil and the noble child was anointed king. The golden robe was put on him. Then the Archbishop took the Holy Crown and put it on the head of the noblest king as is the custom in Christianity today: King Ladislas, the son of King Albert and the grandson of Emperor Sigismund was crowned with the Holy Crown by the Archbishop of Esztergom, in Székesfehérvár on the sacred day of Whitsun.'

Queen Elizabeth knew exactly that after this ceremony her son's claim to the throne was certain even though he was only an infant. She also knew that King Wladislas III (Wladislas I in Hungary), who was requested by the Hungarian noblemen, would not succeed, as the Queen and her son went to Vienna after the coronation and took the crown with them. In her difficult financial situation she put the crown in pawn with Emperor Federick. Only King Matthias was able to get it back. That was the reason why the coronation was so urgent and every element carefully followed. Mrs Kottanner writes: 'After the noble King Ladislas was crowned in my arm at St. Stephen's altar, I took the noble King up some samll stairs on a platform as it was usual. Then the form of oath which belongs to the coronation was read out.' The ritual prescribed a certain type of golden fabric on which the king had to sit, so the King's nurse put the child's red and golden blanket lined with white fur under the King. During the mass Ulrik Cillei held the crown over Ladislas' head. Then as part of the usual ceremony instead of the King Miklós Újlaki knighted some noblemen who were entitled to wear gold spurs after this day. Mrs Kottanner remarks that everybody was surprised by the infant 'who held up his head so strongly that it can rarely be seen from a twelve-week-old child when the Archbishop put the crown over his head.' Later he started to cry and 'people were surprised and said: this is not the voice of a twelve-week-old child, he cried as if he was one year old.'

From the basilica the procession went to St. Peter's Church, and the nurse 'had to take the King out of his cradle and seat him in a chair as it was usual, because every king who was crowned had to sit here.' After these ceremonies the procession walked along the town as this was traditional. 'Only the noble Count Ulrik Cillei was on horseback as he had to hold the Holy Crown over the head of the noble King so that everybody could see it: the Holy Crown, which was put on the heads of the saint king, St. Stephen, and other kings of Hungary.' This means that in the time of Helena Kottanner the Holy Crown was thought to have belonged to St. Stephen. The lords of the country were holding the orb, the sceptre, Cillei's sword, with which the King was knighted, and before the King a cross to symbolize that the country was completely independent from the Holy Roman Empire as the first Hungarian king received the crown from the Pope thus he did not owe allegiance to anyone. The Hungarian royal regalia represented the rights of the king as sovereign, as supreme commander and as advowson (i.e. to appoint prelates). The symbol of the supreme commander was the sword and the flag, the latter was also kept in Székesfehérvár, and in the case of war it was ceremoniously unrolled to symbolize that the king was going to war (just like the famous war flag of the French, Oriflamme). The offices of swordbearer and flagbearer were special positions in the royal court.

Helena Kottanner writes about her own role: 'The noble Queen respected her son so much and was so humble of heart that I, the simple woman, had to go the closest to the noble King before Her Highness, as I had to hold His Majesty in arms.'

So a few-month-old infant ascended the throne, most of the aristocracy supported another sovereign and the Turks were marching towards the border ...

THE HUNGARIAN CROWN

There are conflicting opinions and ideas about the origin of the crown; it is, however, certain that it became the symbol of the Hungarian state very soon. The crown was the most dominant symbol in the Hungarian coronation ceremony and it seems to have had the most important role as opposed to the West-European ritual, in which anointment was the main momentum. The text of the oath is worded as follows: '... (the crown) symbolizes the glory and reverence of holiness ... so that you can reign for long among the glorious decorated with the gems of virtue and crowned with the gratification of eternal happiness'. From the 14th century it was a general rule that the legitimate king of Hungary had to be crowned with the crown said to have belonged to St. Stephen. One of the miniatures of the Illuminated Chronicle depicts a theft of the crown, though it is not mentioned in the text; the most famous theft was accomplished by the lady-in-waiting of Elizabeth, King Albert' widow, Mrs Helena Kottanner, who wrote a diary about it.

CORONATION
OF ANDREW I, *miniature
from the Illuminated
Chronicle.*
The ceremony in the picture depicts an early custom, here the sword symbolizing secular power is handed over to the King by a bishop. This monument of the ritual later became the privilege of secular lords; when Ladislas V was crowned, the Transylvanian Viovode accomplished this with the sword of the King's relative, Urlik Cillei.

CORONATION OF GÉZA II.
*Miniature from the
Illuminated Chronicle.*
One momentum of the inauguration of the new king was to gird him with the sword. This is accomplished here by the brother of the King, Prince Ladislas. The King's horse led up indicates the tradition that the King rides around the town with his retinue to a hill at the egde of the town, where he strokes with the sword to the four cardinal points to symbolize that he protects the country from all enemies.

A ROYAL FUNERAL

King Charles Robert, the King of Hungary, Croatia, Dalmatia, Serbia, Galicia, Ladomeria and Cumania, the ruler of Salerno and St. Angel Hill, died after the reign of forty-one years on 16 July 1342.

The death of a king, just like his life, is never a private matter, his funeral has to match his social status and reflect stateliness and dignity.

The funeral of the first Hungarian king of the House of Anjou met all the requirements and came up to the expectations of the tradition; as is described in Thuróczy chronicle. The chronicle itself dates about a hundred years later, but the text used by Thuróczy was most probably written by a contemporary court historiographer.

The day after the King's death the dignitaries of the country gathered in the castle of Visegrád, which then was the royal seat, to pay tribute to the dead King lying in state, with the crown on his head, in a scarlet suit and boots ornamented with precious stones. Then his body was taken to the town, to St. Mary's parish Church, where the town mourned the King. After the requiem mass the catafalque was taken down to Buda by ship on the Danube; then the body lay in state in the Church of Our Lady. The ecclesiastical and secular dignitaries followed the ship on the bank. The royal standard, which was conveyed in front of Charles Robert in his battles, was also carried on the bank. This banner was generally kept in Székesfehérvár, and was guarded by a special court officer, the 'vexillifer'.

The requiem mass was in the Buda parish church (today Matthias Church) on 18 July, after the body was taken to Buda in a procession the previous night. During the ceremony three knights stood guard outside the doorway, they were wearing the armour of the king. The first knight supposedly was dressed in a hunting-suit, the second in the tilting armour used in tournaments and the third the regimentals of the king. The chronicle writer described them as follows:

'All the harness, bits and bridles were of gilt silver appropriate to the King's dignity, the leather straps and reins and other things including the breast harness and cruppers were covered with silk. The three knights and their horses were clad in purple, with a lot of beautiful embroidery, pearls and precious stones; they were completely similar to the king.'

Then the funeral procession went to Székesfehérvár, where the king was buried beside his predecessors in the royal basilica. The procession must have been similar to the ones when the French kings and princes of Burgundy buried: it consisted of priests and fiars carrying processional crosses and flags, psalmists, prelates robbed in pontificals, lords, hooded mourners like the ones on the tombs of the prices of Burgundy, and the mourning family. The procession was headed by the three knights in their royal suits. They may have replaced the wax figures which were carried in the procession in the town where the burial was done, which can be read about in chronicles reporting about the funeral of French kings.

Charles Robert was buried beside the main altar of the Székesfehérvár basilica, Csanád Telegdi, the archbishop of Esztergom, preached the sermon. After the funeral, as Thuróczy says:

'Finally the three horses with the arms and blankets, the French rolling cart, that is the royal carriage, which was decorated with the gilt and pearled coat of arms, above it a bird like an ortrich and seven gilt spheres also made of silver, ... were donated to the monastery mentioned.'

The 'monastery mentioned' was the chapter of Székesfehérvár, the carriage-like thing was the King's coach ornamented with the royal coat of arms: the dexter striped with silver and red of the House of Árpád, and the blue sinister with the golden fleur de lis of the House of Anjou, above them the ostrich biting a horse shoe, which was considered as the crest of the Hungarian kings; it is desribed like this in several western books on coats of arms.

After the royal funerals the 'requisites' were generally given to the church which had performed the ceremony.

Charles Robert's wife, Elizabeth mentioned several ecclesiastical bodies — which celebrated Mass for her — in her will, which included some bequeasts to them some.

As for the three knights, an old special Hungarian custom was also used in this part of the funeral ceremony. It is a well-known fact that among the grave-goods of the conquering Hungarians the remains of the saddle horses used in battles, which were killed at the funeral, can also be found.

We have data about this custom, though in a changed form, from the 12th century: between 1177 and 1192 the parents of a student who died in Paris left money for the funeral, among other things for flags, clothes and a white horse. All this was recorded in a letter of the abbey of St. Genevieve's Church in Paris. We have further data from c 1270: in his will Demeter, the son of Beszter, wished that on the day of his death his best horse fully harnessed and with his armour should be led in the funeral procession, then bestowed to the Franciscan friary of St. John in Buda. Several other examples could be mentioned from the 15th—16th centuries which prove that this custom — i.e. the presentation of the horse and its armour of the deceased in the funeral procession — was widespread among the members of the aristocracy as well.

Thirty days after the funeral the mourners participated in a solemn Mass, then funeral feast also in Székesfehérvár, 'where the body of King Charles was ceremoniously buried, here and in the town of Visegrád the Queen and her kind son, Luis, already crowned king, piously celebrated the memorial service with prelates, bishops, priests and barons and many-many Christian believers. And all the people of the country celebrated the memorial services with the same religious devotion.' — finishes the description Thuróczy.

SILVER FUNERAL CROWN *from Margaret Island.* The silver crown with lilies was found in one of the graves opened up in the territory of the Dominican convent on Margaret Island. It must have belonged to Stephen V. The royal regalia was symbolically placed in the graves, which was the custom during the Middle Ages.

THE FUNERAL OF KING ST. LADISLAS *from the Illustrated Chronicle.*
Before his death King Ladislas declared his will that he wanted to be buried in Nagyvárad: in spite of his wish the funeral procession was going to Székesfehérvár. Legend has it that one morning the pallbearers noticed that the carriage carrying the body had disappeared; it was found on the road to Nagyvárad, as it was advancing by itself. Later Queen Mary and her husband, Sigismund, the sovereign of the Holy Roman Empire were also buried beside the tomb of St. Ladislaus in Nagyvárad.

CHRONOLOGY

c. 900	After his army invades Pannonia, Chieftain Árpád settles where later the town of Székesfehérvár is founded.
972—997	St. Peter's Church, the burial place of Prince Géza and his wife, Adelheid is built.
1002	The name of the town is Alba Civitas in the deed of foundation of the Veszprém bishopric.
1007	Prince Emeric (later St. Emeric) is born in the royal palace in Székesfehérvár.
c. 1018	King Stephen moves his seat from Esztergom to Székesfehérvár. The building of the royal basilica founded by King Stephen begins.
1031	Prince Emeric is buried.
1038	King Stephen is buried.
1044	In the Jerusalem itinerary the town is mentioned as Wyzenburg (Weisenburg).
1045	Henry III, Emperor of the Holy Roman Empire occupies Székesfehérvár to help Peter Orseolo ascend the throne.
1046	Andrew I is crowned king in Székesfehérvár, his soldiers blind the returning King Peter, who dies in captivity.
1051	The troops of Henry III advance as far as Székesfehérvár but are unable to occupy the town.
1055	The Hungarian name of the town, 'Feheruuaru' is first mentioned in the Tihany deed of foundation.
1060	Béla is crowned king in Székesfehérvár.
1061	Béla I summons a nationwide meeting in Székesfehérvár.
1077—1095	The market and fairs of the town are mentioned.
1083	King Stephen I then his son Prince Emeric are canonized in the royal basilica.
1096	The crusaders crossing Székesfehérvár call the town as 'Bellegrava', the centre of the country. They also mention St. Martin's Church in the suburb.
c. 1100	'Codex Albensis', the oldest manuscript in Hungary with musical notation and a Latin poem praising St. Stephen is copied.
1116	Coloman Beauclerc is buried, his son Stephen II is crowned in the royal basilica
1131	Béla the Blind is crowned in Székesfehérvár.
1141	Béla the Blind is buried in the royal basilica.
c. 1151	Mastyrius, the Archbishop of Esztergom, founds and with the help of Queen Eufrosina builds a convent in Székesfehérvár in honour of St. Mary for the crusadors. The beginning of the 12th c. St. Nicolas' Collegiate Chapter is probably built, but is first mentioned only in 1215.
1162	Géza II is buried in Székesfehérvár.
1163	Ladislas II is buried in Székesfehérvár. Stephen III defeats Stephen IV's army near the town.
1165	Stephen IV is buried in Székesfehérvár.
1185	Béla III keeps St. Stephen's celebration in Székesfehérvár, royal assizes are mentioned first.
1192	St. Stephen's Church, hospice and hospital owned by the Hospitallers in Szentkirályföld are first mentioned.
1196	Béla III is buried beside his first wife in the royal basilica; his son, Emeric is crowned.
1205	Ladislas III is buried.
1221	The friary and St. Margaret's Church of the Dominican are founded in the new town.
1233	The salt-office in Székesfehérvár is first mentioned.

1234	Andrew II enters into a marriage contract with his third wife, Beatrix Este in Székesfehérvár. The hospital of St. Nicolas' Chapter is mentioned.	1303	According to a charter the Augustinians build a friary in a suburb.
1235	Béla IV is crowned.	1310	Charles Robert's (third) coronation with the Holy Crown in Székesfehérvár.
1237	Béla IV confirms the rights of the town: the body of magistrates consists of 1 judge and 12 jurymen.	1317	Queen Mary is buried in the royal basilica.
1242	After an unsuccessful siege againt Székesfehérvár the Mongols set the Budai (?) suburb on fire.	1318	Charles Robert vaults the royal basilica.
		1327	The suburb, Sziget, later Újváros, is first mentioned. The royal basilica burns down.
1249	Béla IV settles the 'Latins' in the territory of the early royal castle. Ramparts, a new palace and castle and the present street system are built.	1328	The treasurer is mentioned to measure 50 pounds of Viennese denarius according to the Székesfehérvár weight, in György Györffy's view this suggests that a mint worked here.
1260	The Franciscan friary and church is already built in the Budai suburb.	1329	Judge Markus issues a charter.
1263	The church of the Holy Cross in the inner town, which was already finished at the beginning of the 11th c., is firt mentioned.	1331	The Budai suburb, which was already populated earlier, is first mentioned.
		1342	Charles Robert is buried, Luis I (the Great) is crowned in Székesfehérvár.
1270	Stephen V and his wife, Elizabeth are crowned.	1352	Luis the Great convenes the parliament to Székesfehérvár.
1272	Some lords led by Egyed from the Monoszló family attack the Székesfehérvár house of the widowed Queen Elizabeth. Szentkirályföld possessed by the Hospitallers is first mentioned.	1381	St. Peter utca (street) in the inner town is first mentioned.
		1382	Luis I is buried in the side chapel of the royal basilica.
1276	St. Mary's convent of the Dominican nuns in the Budai suburb is first mentioned.	1387	Sigismund of Luxemburg is crowned in Székesfehérvár. Vicus Magnus, the Main Street in the inner town is first mentioned.
1288	The town, the royal basilica and the outer 'chamber' burn down.	1394	Sziget utca in the suburb is first mentioned.
1290	The decree of Andrew III oders that the judges and lords are to hold annual sessions in Székesfehérvár.	1403	Sigismund convenes the parliament to Székesfehérvár.
		1405	Borbala Cillei is crowned Queen.
1298	The southern suburb of Székesfehérvár, Újfalu, is first mentioned.	1436	Sigismund receives the legates of the Czech estates in Székesfehérvár.
1299	Andrew III holds a parliamentary session in Székesfehérvár.	1437	St. Elizabeth' Church in the suburb is first mentioned.
		1438	Albert is crowned.

1440	The infant Ladislas is crowned with the stolen crown, later Wladislas I is crowned. The Székesfehérvár parliament issues Wladislas' decree.	1506	Ann is buried in the royal basilica.
1445	The magnates confer in Székesfehérvár.	1508	The heir to the throne, Luis is crowned.
1446	The parliament is meeting is Székesfehérvár.	1510	The parliament meets in Székesfehérvár.
1464	Matthias is crowned at the Székesfehérvár parliament.	1514	The vineyards of the town are mentioned.
1473	Matthias fortifies the ramparts with bastions.	1516	Wladislas II is buried in Székesfehérvár.
1476	Székesfehérvár litigates about taxes on markets together with other towns	1521	Mary of Hapsburg is crowned.
1485	King Matthias builds his sepulchral chapel in the rampart.	1526	Luis II is buried between Wladislas II and St. Emeric. John of Szapolya, Transylvanian voivode convenes the parliament to Székesfehérvár.
1490	King Matthias is buried in the side chapel of the royal basilica. Maximilian, Roman king occupies Székesfehérvár.	1527	Ferdinand I is crowned.
1491	István Báthory and Pál Kinizsi reoccupy the town.	1540	John I is buried in Székesfehérvár. Leonhard Vels occupies the town.
1502	Wladislas II marries Ann Candale.	1541	The Turkish troops are close to Székesfehérvár, the ramparts are fortified.
		1543	Sultan Suleiman occupies Székesfehérvár.

BIBLIOGRAPHY

Árpád-kori legendák és intelmek (Árpádian legends and admonitions) Selected by Géza Érszegi. Budapest 1983.

Dercsényi, Dezső: A székesfehérvári Királyi bazilika (The Székesfehérvár Royal basilica) Budapest 1943.

Dormuth, Árpád: Adatok a városháza múltjához. (Data to the past of the town hall) Székesfehérvári Szemle 1937. pp 18—23.

Dormuth, Árpád: A várfal alapjának maradványai (The remains of the ramparts in the yard of the museum) Székesfehérvári Szemle 1935. pp 89—90.

Érszegi, Géza: Fejér megyére vonatkozó oklevelek a székesfehérvári keresztes konvent levéltárában, 1193—1542 (Charters concerning the Fejér county in the archives of the convent of Székesfehérvár crusaders, 1193—1542) Fejér megyei Történeti Évkönyv 5. 1971. pp 177—263.

Fitz, Jenő: A középkori Székesfehérvár. (The medieval Székesfehérvár) István Király Múzeum Közleményei B. 11. Székesfehérvár, 1956. p 25.

Fitz, Jenő: A székesfehérvári Budai külváros középkori templomai. (The medieval churches of the Budai suburb in Székesfehérvár) IKMK A. 3. 1956. p 13.

Fitz, Jenő—Császár, László—Papp, Imre: Székesfehérvár. Budapest 1966. p 158.

Fügedi, Erik: Székesfehérvár középkori alaprajza és a polgárság kezdetei Magyarországon (The plan of the medieval Székesfehérvár) Településtudományi Közlemények 20. 1967. p 34.

Györffy, György: Az Árpád-kori Magyarország történeti földrajza II. (The historical geography of the Árpádian Hungary II) Budapest 1987. p 363.

Károly, János: Fejér vármegye története II. (The history of the Fejér county II) Székesfehérvár 1898. p 717.

Kovács, Péter: Megjegyzések Székesfehérvár középkori topográfiájának kutatásához (Some remarks to the research of the medieval topography of Székesfehérvár) Alba Regia XII. 1971. pp 261—267.

Kralovánszky, Alán: Baukunsthistorische Angaben zur Frage des Auftauchens des vierapsidalen Kirchentyps in Ungarn. Folia Archaeologica XXXV. Budapest 1984. 111—138.

Kralovánszky, Alán: The earliest church of Alba Civitas. Alba regia XX. 1983. pp 35—89.

Kralovánszky, Alán: Székesfehérvár kialakulása a régészeti adatok alapján. (The development of Székesfehérvár) Székesfehérvár Évszázadai 1. pp 7—18.

Kralovánszky, Alán: Székesfehérvár. Királyi bazilika I—II. (Székesfehérvár. The royal basilica) Tájak-Korok-Múzeumok Kiskönyvtára, 309—310. sz. 1988.

Mezey, László: Székesfehérvár egyházi intézményei a középkorban. (The ecclesiastical institutions in Székesfehérvár in the Middle Ages) Székesfehérvár Évszázadai 2. 1972. pp 21—26.

Nagy, Lajos: Székesfehérvár későközépkori topográfiája. (The late medieval topography of Székesfehérvár) Székesfehérvár Évszázadai 2. 1972. pp 199—214.

Siklósi, Gyula: A fehérvári királyi bazilika. (The royal basilica in Székesfehérvár) Múzsák Magazin 1992/2. XXIII. 2. pp 3—5.

Siklósi, Gyula: Adattár Székesfehérvár középkori és törökkori épitészetéről. (Data about the medieval and Turkish architecture of Székesfehérvár) Székesfehérvár 1990. p 116.

Siklósi, Gyula: Angaben zur mittelalterichen Topographie von Székesfehérvár aufgrund der Grundrisse und Kasten über die Stadt. Acta Archealogica Tom. XL. fasc. 1—4. 1988. pp 211—250.

Siklósi, Gyula: A székesfehérvári korai és későbbi királyi vár illetve palota. (The early and late royal castle and palace) Castrum Bene 1989. Gyöngyös 1990. pp 104—120.

Siklósi, Gyula: A székesfehérvári Szent Bertalan templom. (St. Bartholomew's Church in Székesfehérvár) Alba Regia XXIV. 1990. pp 141—149.

Siklósi, Gyula: Neuere Forschungen im Árpádenzeitlichen Székesfehérvár. Acta Archaelogica 44. 1992. pp 371—388.

Siklósi, Gyula: Székesfehérvár legkorábbi egyházi intézményei a középkorban. (The earliest ecclesiastical institutions of Székesfehérvár) Egyházak a változó világban. Edited by István Bárdos and Margit Beke. Esztergom, 1991. pp 109—118.

Siklósi, Gyula—Hadházi, Gábor: A székesfehérvári királyi bazilikához tartozó kolostor (Vasvári P. u. 3.) feltárása (The excavation of the monastery belonging to the Székesfehérvár royal basilica) Manuscript 1993.

Varjú, Elemér: Szent István koporsója. (St. Stephen's coffin) Magyar Művészet 6. 1930. pp 372—379.

Veress, D. Csaba—Siklósi, Gyula: Székesfehérvár, a királyok városa (Székesfehérvár, the town of kings) Budapest, 1990. p 277.

THE OPENING HOURS OF THE MUSEUMS

István király Múzeum
8000 Székesfehérvár, Fő ucta 6.
Archaelogical exhibition
Open: 10 am—to 4 pm,
closed on Monday.

Királyi bazilika: ruins
8000 Székesfehérvár, Koronázó tér 1.
Open: 9 am—6 pm from April to October, closed on Monday

ÓBUDA

GEOGRAPHICAL CONDITIONS

In the formation of settlements geographical conditions have a decisive role. The most important factors are the nearness of water and the choice of the area suitable for animal husbandry and farming. The medieval Óbuda developed on the right bank of the River Danube, on a respectively narrow stretch of land satisfying all these demands. In the Danube there are some islands here, so it lends itself particularly well for crossing the river. The obvious routes also led here, it was possible to cross the Danube between the Great Plain and Transdanubia at this crossing place.

THE ROMAN HERITAGE

In the Roman times the centre of the Pannonia province, the legionary camp and town of Aquincum were built here. The Roman ruins remained for centuries, at the time of the Hungarian conquest they may have been quite tall, and some parts of some buildings were reused even during the Middle Ages. The Roman network of roads, which used the favourable geographical conditions and the obvious routes, may have been in a relatively good condition.

THE TIME OF THE HUNGARIAN CONQUEST

The conquering Hungarian tribes and families occupied the eastern part of the Carpatian Basin first about 895; then they crossed the Danube here, at the present Óbuda; and by about 900 they took up Transdanubia, i.e. the territory of the Roman Pannonia. The conquering Hungarians had two princes: 'gyula', who had the actual power and 'kündü', who was the sacral prince. Kündü Kurszán shared the governing with Prince Árpád; and the placename 'Castrum Curzan' can be found even in a 14th century charter, which refers to the fact that the kündü resided in Óbuda during the Hungarian conquest. Historical research identified Kurszan's castle with the Roman military amphitheatre in today's Nagyszombat utca.

Kurszan was killed at a feast in 902 or 904; after his death Árpád exercised the power alone. He occupied the dwelling place of the kündü, and scattered his people to guard the borders. The fact that in 907 Árpád was buried in the hillside over the today's Óbuda also shows that he acquired land here. Later the royal chapel of Fejéregyháza was founded here in honour of the founder of the dynasty. So Óbuda was a princely centre from the time of the Hungarian conquest, and kept this role during the Middle Ages.

THE AGE OF THE HOUSE OF ÁRPÁD

In the last third of the 10th century Prince Géza moved his seat to Esztergom. This may have been one of the reasons that Óbuda was not involved in the centralized organization of counties and the Church in the time of Saint Stephen.

During the formation of the structure of the royal estate there may have stood a royal mansion here, which was the economic centre that collected the crop of the serfs living on the royal estates in the neighbourhood.

We look for the Fejéregyháza, also called Bánya St. Mary parish Church and the royal mansin in its vicinity on the west side of today's Bécsi út in the hillside over Óbuda. In spite of the fact that Óbuda was left out of King Stephan's activities to establish the state and the Church, our chronicles attribute to him the foundation of the ecclesiastical institution, the collegiate chapter, which was of outstanding importance in the development of the town. According to sources it is more likely that it was his successor, Peter of Venice (1038—1041, 1044—1046), who founded the provostry consecrated to Apostle Saint Peter. The construction was finished by St. Ladislaus (1077—1095), who also funded the church. In the 11th century independently of the founder this ecclesiastical institution played a very significant role in the development of the town.

The medieval town — which was called Buda till the middle of the 13th century — developed from double—cored settlement centres. In its northern part the 'civitas', the ecclesiastical centre of the town, the provostry was built. Besides the church this ecclesiastical centre included the palace of the provost, the houses of the members of the ecclesiastical board and those of the servants as well as farm—buildings. These building complexes are being looked for in the present Fő tér and its vicinity; some part have already been found here during the recent archaelogical research.

In the south—eastern part of the 'civitas' a ferry began to work in the Middle Ages, this connected the commercial routes and also ensured the crossing over the Danube. The market here became the centre of unloading goods transported by water and also that of commerce; and the money from the customs and ferry was a very significant source of income for the king. Around the port and the roads leading there a settlement of craftsmen and merchants was built. The village, 'villa' was to be found in the area which is bordered today by Kiskorona utca and Árpádfejedelem útja. The two cores of the settlement remained different during the Middle Ages.The 13th—century charters also mention 'villa' and 'civitas'; the inhabitants of the 'villa' were 'hospes' and 'cives', i.e. settlers and burghers, those of the 'civitas' were 'custodes regie domus' and 'familiis iobagionem, comitum videlicet et prelatorum' , i.e. the guards and serfs of the royal mansion, respectively the household of the bailiffs and the prelates.

The rich endowments given already by St. Ladislaus show that there was a close relationship between the royal court and provosts. This was confirmed in a charter issued by King Géza II in 1148; this is the first charter, which describes the borders of (Ó)Buda. From the second part of the 12th century the provosts of the church are already mentioned among the high dignitaries right after the bishops; and in 1186 Adorján was both the provost and the royal chancellor. Historical research considers it very likely that Master P., the notary of King Béla III (1172—1196), also called Anonymus, the author of the 'Gesta Hungarorum' was the member of both the chancellery and the church. The close contact of the chancellery and the provostry suggests that the King must have stayed here for a longer period of time.

It is well—known from the description of Ansbert and Arnold of Lübeck accompanying Emperor Frederick Barbarossa (Red—bearded), who participated in the third crusade, that King Béla III and his wife (Margaret Capet, the sister of the French king,

Philip II) escorted the Emperor to (Ó)Buda after the reception in Esztergom; then entertained him on his own hunting—fields (today the Csepel Island) for another two days. As the Emperor continued his journey to the east, and sent legates back to King Béla, whom they found in (Ó)Buda at Christmas. Obviously there must have been a royal mansion which was worthy to receive the Emperor, and was big enough for him and his escort. This building is most probably to be found near the provostry.

The importance of the commerce which now expanded to great distances promoted the town as well. So during the reign of Emeric (1196—1204) and Andrew II (1205—1235) the royal estates and letters—patent were started to be bestowed.

King Emeric also made a generous donation to the Buda provostry. Though Endre II withdrew it when he ascended the throne in 1205, but gave it back in 1212. According to this the provostry in Buda received the town with its wine taxes, market customs and the right to administer justice. The charter also describes the borders of the town, but it is very difficult to identify them with the present place—names. The town must have stretched from the present Szépvölgy deep in the hills along the Hármashatárhegy and Aranyhegy and down to the Danube near the present Roman Bath.

The fact that the market customs and wine taxes were given away shows that (Ó)Buda was of less importance as a royal seat during the reign of Emeric and Andrew II.

At the end of the 12th and at the beginning of the 13th centuries the economic boom resulted in the significant development of the craftsmen and merchants as well as the market. The market place was first mentioned in a deed of gift in 1212, which says that its income was also given to the provostry. The archaelogical research uncovered the market place of the town in the area among the following streets of today: Árpádfejedelem útja, Lajos utca and Tél utca. The more or less triangular market place must have been along the north—eastern — south—western roads, which connected the ferry and the main road leading to Esztergom. The market place was already lined with stone houses at the turn of the 12—13th centuries.

There is data about the donation of (Ó)Buda, but there is no about when one part of the town belonged to the royal estates again and when the new royal castle was started to be constructed. It is possible that when in 1198 King Emeric handed over the Esztergom castle to the archbishop, the kings gradually left the castle; thus it was necessary to build a new castle in Buda. The charters dated in Buda say that from the second decade of the 13th century Andrew II already stayed in his own Buda mansion at Easter — Quadragesima; and he had the spring royal assizes and judical sessions here. King Béla IV (1235—1270) regularly spent the Lent here; and after he ascended the throne he liked staying in Buda. This second royal castle was uncovered under and near the present Calvinist church and parish at 2—4 Kalvin köz. The symmetrical castle with a square plan was built at the south—western corner of the town at the edge of the built—in area in the first third of the 13th century. The castle is mentioned as the centre of the country, which means both a natural, geographical and an administrative centre as well.

Buda took the first steps on the road to becoming a capital, but this was prevented by the Mongol invasion in 1241—1242 and its consequences. The town, which had no ramparts, was immediately captured in the Mongol attack; and Batu khan stayed here before advancing against Esztergom.

When the Mongol army left in the spring of 1242, the country was in ruins. St. Peter's Church of the provostry in (Ó)Buda was also ruined, only its chancel was repaired, the church itself was not rebuilt; obviously the other parts of the town were ruined as well.

The inhabitants of the town returned; and the rebuilding and development started.

St. Margaret's Chapel, which belonged to the Fejéregyháza royal chapel, became the parish church of the town.

Wine growing, agriculture, animal husbandry and fishing in the Danube formed the economic background of the reviving town. Agricultural goods were processed here as well: there were water mills, and several bakers, butchers and smiths lived in the town.

It refers to the flourishing town life that in the north—western edge of the town, in the present Vöröskereszt utca, a Franciscan church and friary were built.

The Mongol invasion could not destroy the castles and towns surrounded with walls; so more and more settlements were fortified. One of these was the Castle Hill (Várhegy) in Buda, so the people moved there from (Ó)Buda and Pest.

From the middle of the 13th century the place—name 'Buda' refers to the new settlement on the Várhegy; and the one called 'Buda' so far was mentioned as 'Vetus Buda' — Óbuda first in 1261.

The Óbuda provosts still called themselves the Buda provost during the Middle Ages. The provostry was entrusted with notorial functions, which denoted the presence of the royal court. In the 13th century the charters dated in 'Buda' were actually written in the (Ó)Buda castle, which functioned as a royal seat. In 1288 King Ladislas IV and in 1296 the wife of King Andrew III, Agnes Hapsburg, mentioned their permanent residence in Óbuda. After the death of King Andrew III, the last king of the House of Árpád, in 1301 the Queen gave the Óbuda royal palace to the magnates.

However, the royal court gradually moved to the castle built on Várhegy, and thus so did the officials and the nobility as well as the craftsmen and merchants around the royal court. This meant that the most important people in the development of a town left Óbuda.

14TH—16TH CENTURIES

When King Luis the Great (1342—1382) endowed the Óbuda castle to his mother, Elizabeth Piast in 1343, the town started to develop again. From this time on the castle belonged to the queens. The widowed Queen Elizabeth arranged her residence here, and also had some reconstruction done.

Queen Elizabeth is associated with the most enormous Gothic construction in Óbuda. She had the church and convent of the Poor Claire built for her and her parents salvation in the area bordered today by Kiskorona utca, Perc utca and Mókus utca. The building work was done in the 1340s after the papal permission was given in 1334. The Queen made a generous donation to the convent; and in 1380 according to her will she was buried in the Corpus Christi Chapel built near the church. Later the convent became the centre of education of aristocratic girls.

Beside the St. Peter's Church of the provostry, which was still in ruins, she also had another church built together with her son, King Luis the Great; this was finished by 1348 and consecrated to St.Mary, its beauty was long admired.

There were constant conflicts about the ownership of Óbuda among the provosts and the castellans of the kings and later the queens. King Luis the Great settled the dispute over the judical, ecclesiastical and proprietary rights so that he divided the town between the provost and the Queen in 1355. The charter issued about this is of special importance from the point of view of the historical research, as it describes the borders of the town: the border of the down-town began at the present Roman bath, stretched towards the south along the pillars of the Roman aque-duct in the line of the present Szentendrei út, near the mansion of the Franciscans, the gate of which looked onto Fejéregyháza, where it reached the actual town. The road led across the grange of the Queen as far as the castle; the borderline between the quarter of the provost in the north and that of the Queen in the south was indicated here. Then the road passing the castle led to the Danube, and crossing it reached the north end of the Margaret Island, where the castle of the archbishop was to be found.

The fact that King Luis the Great divided Óbuda confirmed the existing differences.

In the northern, ecclesiastical quar-ter the provost owned the wine taxes and right of exercising judical powers. In the quarter of the Queen burghers were headed by a council with con-siderable rights to govern. They were entitled to issue charters with the seal of the town in affairs concerning the town. St. Margaret's Chapel became the parish church, and was enlarged with a side—chapel whose walls have been found on the south side of the present Roman Catholic church in Templom utca.

The market place also got into the quarter of the Queen; the houses standing here were rebuilt and enlarged, which has been proved by archaelogical research as well. The buildings in the final, 14th—15th—century—arrangement of the triangu-lar market place showed a scattered development method on the eastern side, i.e. the narrower facades looked onto the place, while on the western side a development in unbroken rows. The customs of the ferry ensur-ing quite a good income was given to the nuns of the Order of Poor Claire.

From 1357 the main duty of the Franciscans was the spiritual instruc-tion of the nuns of the Order of Poor Claire. The importance of the friary standing at the north—western edge of the ecclesiastical quarter grew after 1444, when only one friary remained in the hand of the Conventuals after the Fransiscan Order was divided into two parts: Observant and Conventual. The leader of the Order stayed here more often, and the friary often housed the assemblies of the Order. Unfortunately excavations have only been done in a very small area in today's Vöröskereszt utca, so no evi-dence of any rebuilding has been found so far.

The quarter of the provost remained of ecclesiastical character. The palace of the provost, the houses of the relativaly large number of canons, chapel and altar wardens may have stood in the south—east of the church of the provostry. The parts of the buildings found in Szentlélek tér and its vicinity must have belonged to the houses of Káptalansor (Chapter Lane). The few houses built by burghers must have stood here as well.

The provostry headed often by high rank state officals was still entitled with notorial functions, which was respected in the whole country. The fact that King Sigismund (1387—1437) founded the second university of the country here in 1395 shows that the provostry was of great importance and may have had a very good school. The Óbuda provost, Lukács Szántai was appointed as chancellor of the university. The university ceased to funtion by the end of the 14th century, so King Sigismund founded it again in 1410. It was a real 'universitas'; it had all the four faculties: faculties of teology, ecclesiastical and civil law, medicine and liberal arts. Unfortunately this university did not exist for a long time either; it closed down the latest when Sigismund died.

King Matthias Hunyadi (1458—1490) asked for the Pope's permission in 1483 to demolish the St. Peter's Church of the provostry standing in ruins to be able to found and build a friary for the Order of Saint Paul from its stones to support the Fejéregyháza church consecrated to the St. Mary. The remains of the friary complex, which was at the present 166 Bécsi út, were most probably destroyed at the end of the last century, when the Victoria brick—factory was built.

The burghers of Óbuda, which was under the control of two landlords, lost the possibility to acquire the rights of a town in legal and economic respects.

By the middle of the 14th century most of the royal administration, merchants and very likely a part of the craftsmen left; and this meant the decay of the town. It was rather a country town where mainly wine growers owning houses in the town and quite a large number of butchers lived. The sources do not mention any industry or commerce large in scale. In the 15th—16th centuries Óbuda was not able to advance to the rank of a town; only the beauty and the size of its ecclesiastical buildings were remarkable.

The town without ramparts was defenceless against the attacks of the Turks. The Turkish army reaching Buda destroyed Óbuda as well in 1526. The inhabitants fled, then some of them returned. In 1541 Óbuda — together with Buda and Pest — got under Turkish rule for about 150 years, and this meant the devastation of the medieval town.

SILVER SIGNET OF ÓBUDA,
the middle of the 14th century.

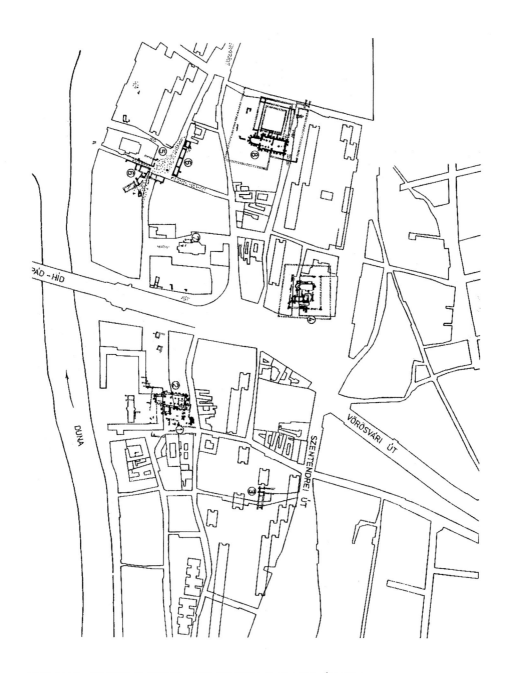

THE MAP OF THE DOWNTOWN OF THE TODAY'S ÓBUDA *with the medieval parts marked:*
1. St. Peter's Church, 2. St. Mary's Church, 3. Franciscan church and friary, 4. The castle of the kings, later queens, 5. Market place, 6. Houses in the market place, 7. St. Margaret Chapel, 8. The church and convent of the Order of Poor Claire

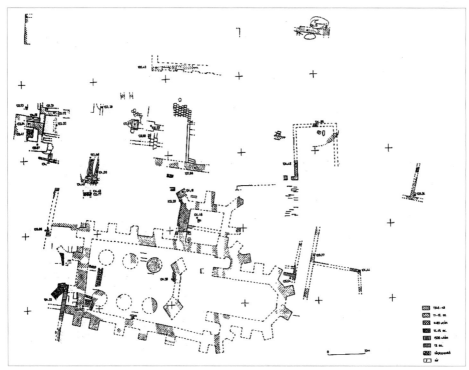

THE GLOBAL PLAN OF THE ARCHAELOGICAL DIG IN THE PRESENT FŐ TÉR
In the chronicle the foundation of the St. Peter's Church of the chapter is attributed to
St. Stephen, though the founder was most probably his successor, Peter. St. Ladislas
made a generous donation, thus he made it possible to finish the construction. The
collegiate chapter founded by the King was directly under the control of the
Archbishop of Esztergom, and was entrusted with notorial functions.
The remains of the St. Peter's Church were probably found in the north part of the
square.
The plan of the second church of the provostry consecrated to St. Mary is in the south
part of the square: a three–aisled church, 60 m long, 20 m wide. Its lengthened chancel
was closed with five sides of the octogon just like those of the aisles. A 10 m wide
cross–aisle joined to the chancels, the nave of the church is divided by four pillars with
arches. On the western facade between two buttresses a tower was built in the second
period. In the 15th century a sacristy was added to the church on the northern side.
The plans besides St. Mary are uncovered remains of the medieval buildings in the
square.

ST. STEPHEN
AND QUEEN GISELA,
Illuminated Chronicle

KING LUIS THE GREAT *as portayed in the Illuminated Chronicle*

SURFACE WITH STONE TILES,
*most possibly the floor covering
of St. Peter's Church.*

ASHLER—WALLED BUILDING
reconstructed several times, in the north—western part of the square.

DETAIL OF AN ASHLER—WALLED
BUILDING *13th century*

CAPITAL DECORATED WITH
ACANTHUS LEAVES
*from the St. Peter's Church,
the beginning of the 12th century.*

DETAIL OF A DOORWAY
OR ROOD—SCREEN
*from St. Peter's Church,
depicting animal fights, the middle
of the 12th century.*

FRAGMENTS OF A RED MARBLE FONT
from St. Mary's Church, the second half of the 15th century

KING BÉLA IV
portayed in the Illuminated Chronicle.

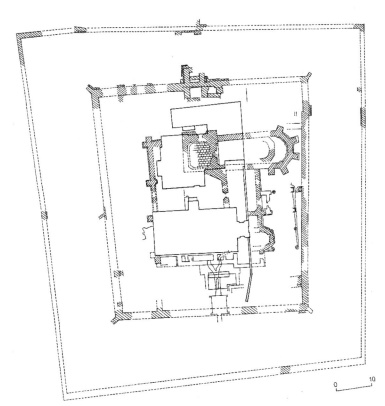

0   10

THE GLOBAL PLAN OF THE ARCHAELOGICAL DIG OF THE CASTLE OF THE
KINGS, LATER THE QUEENS *at 2—4 Kalvin köz*
The castle was built in the 13th—14th centuries. The walls of the castle surrounded an
area of 60 m by 60 m, together with the outer walls the territory of the castle was 100 m
by 100 m. The entrance to the castle led across a bridge on the north side. The square
buildings enclosed an inner yard where richly decorated gates opened from the east and
west buildings. On the eastern side St. Elizabeth' Chapel of the palace protruded from
the the block of the buildings .

ST. ELIZABETH' CHAPEL OF THE CASTLE,
the Romanesque and Gothic chancel during the excavation

QUEEN ELIZABETH WITH HER CHILDREN *in the Illuminated Chronicle*

13TH—CENTURY CARVED STONE FROM THE CASTLE

THE TOMB
OF THE ÓBUDA CASTELLAN,
BERNARDINO MONELLI
FROM 1496

ASHLER—WALLED VAULT
IN THE CHANCEL OF THE CHURCH

THE FRANCISCAN FRIARY
AND CHURCH CONSECRATED
TO ST. FRANCIS
in the present Vöröskereszt utca

The friary was founded in the second half of the 13th century. From the middle of the 14th century the main duty of the Franciscans was the spiritual instruction of the nuns of the Order of Poor Claire. The importance of the friary grew after 1444, when it became the main friary of the Conventuals. During the excavations only a smaller part of the church was found together with the joining eastern wing of the friary.

DECORATED PORTAL WITH
THE JOINING LAYERS OF THE ROAD,
the beginning of the 13th century,
Lajos utca

158. LAJOS UTCA DURING
THE RESEARCH.
The commercial house was built in several phases during the 13th—14th centuries.

THE RECONSTRUCTED BUILDING AT
158. LAJOS UTCA, now the exibition hall of the Budapest Galéria.

THE TOMB OF HENRIK MEHLMAIS-
TER, *the rector the Óbuda university.*

THE COAT OF ARMS OF THE ÓBUDA UNI-
VERSITY *from Ulric Riehental's chronicle written
about the Council of Constance, from 1416*

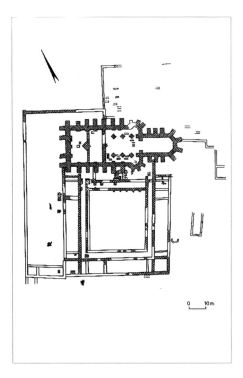

THE PLAN OF THE CHURCH AND CONVENT OF THE ORDER OF POOR CLAIRE   according to the dig in the area bordered by Kiskorona utca — Perc utca — Mókus utca. The church and the convent of the Order of Poor Claire were founded by Queen Elizabeth for her and her parents salvation in 1334. The church has three aisles, and is 60 m long and 20 m wide. The chancel of the nave was closed with five sides of the octogon, just like the aisles. The 20 m by 20 m choir for the nuns was on the west side of the nave. The convent joined to the church in the south. The entrance to the church was in the north side, where the cemetery was to be found. The two—aisled chapter house was in the east wing of the convent, and the refectory, the dining hall of the nuns, in the south wing.

The Corpus Christi Chapel was built in the north part of the cloister, in the south side of the church, where according to her will Queen Elizabeth was buried in 1380.

A BOSS DECORATED WITH LEAVES AND A MASK *from the church, from the middle of the 14th century*

THE CHURCH OF THE ORDER OF POOR CLAIRE *during the excavation*

THE CHURCH AND CONVENT OF THE ORDER OF POOR CLAIRE *after the reconstruction*

KING BÉLA IV IN ÓBUDA

On 17th of February 1241, during Lent Óbuda, which then was only called Buda, witnessed a big and splendid gathering. As it had been usual for a long time, the kings of Hungary spent this time of the year in his residence here to exercise his judical powers. The king had had the right to administer justice over the noblemen of the country since the beginning of the kingdom; earlier, however, the litigants submitted their petitions orally to the king when he ascended the throne, Béla IV ordered that every case had to be handed in in writing to the crown office functioning since Béla III. Master Rogerius writes about this in the sixth chapter of his work 'Miserable Song':

'They very often complained that the King, in spite of the customary law of the country and in order to oppress them, ordered that the noblemen even the high—ranking ones could not start their litigation in his court, and could not speak about their complaints, but had to hand in petitions to the chancellors, and would have to expect them to finish their cases. So many of them had to stay in the court to arrange their pettiest cases for such a long time that they had to sell their horses and other belongings to be able to cover the costs; and very often had to leave without arranging the matters. Because — as they kept saying — some were neglected, some were favoured by the chancellors but without them it was impossible to speak to the King.'

The King probably intended to facilitate the development of literacy and at the same time increase his prestige as well. Béla, who ruled from 1235, wanted to make it obvious for everybody in other fields as well that he literally wished to keep the prestige of the throne. Once he had all the chairs but his throne taken out from his Óbuda mansion and the Esztergom palace. As Master Rogerius reports about this:

'To oppress the bold impertinence of the barons the King ordered that if anyone dared to sit down in his presence — except for the princes, archbishops and bishops — they would have to suffer a worthy punishment. At the same time he had the chairs of the barons, which were found, burned.' So no one was allowed to take a seat in the presence of the King. It was only possible to submit any kind of petition through the crown office even for the dignitaries. All this tension was increased by the suspicion the dignitaries regarded the King, as after his father's death he imprisoned and sent into exile some of his father's supporters among them palatines, the Lord Chief Justice and the Treasurer. Perhaps the enemies of the King considered the Cuman people living in the country to cause all the problems.

The Cuman people arrived in Hungary at Easter of 1239, their number is estimated at forty—thousand by research. The King already had information about the people from which the Cuman people escaped; and suspected that his country would not be able to avoid the diaster, the conquering Mongol horde. To strengthen his army he wanted to use the Cuman horsemen, who fought in the same style as the Mongols, so they meant significant help. Béla also took into consideration the advice of the Dominican friars, who performed missionary activities in the areas where the Cuman people lived. According to Rogerius, Kötöny, the king of the Cuman people, gave the following reasons for and conditions of their settlement in the country:

'He was fighting against the Mongols for several years, and gained a victory twice, but the third time as he was not prepared, he was defeated, and the Mongols quickly occupied his lands. So he had to escape from the disastrous Mongols, who devastated and ransacked most of his lands and killed his subjects. So if King Béla was willing to receive him and leave his freedom, Kötöny would be ready to submit himself to Béla; and move to Hungary with his relatives and friends and all their belongings, and follow the Catholic faith.'

The life of the Cuman people in Hungary was not without frictions, though there is some exaggeration in the contemporary descriptions. It is a fact, however, that the King gave them a lot of lands, which must have interferred with the interests of the Hungarians; and it is also true that the Cuman people was not really able to cope with their new way of life, i.e. being settled. Rogerius says: 'and when the King Kötöny started to wander around in Hungary with his noblemen and commoners with their herds of cattle, they caused a lot of damage to the Hungarians in their fields, gardens, orchards, vineyards and other goods.'

By the end of 1240 it already became obvious that the Mogol horde would soon attack Hungary. The Grand Duke of Kiev had already escaped from his ransacked country, and so had the sovereigns of Vladimir and Galicia. They all came to Hungary. So the King had more and more information about the movements of the Mongol horde. The right wing headed for Poland, the left for Transylvania, while the main body of the army for the middle of the country through the Pass of Verecke.

The size of of the danger was obvious for the King; but the court dignitaries who gathered in Óbuda did not want to believe that the country would soon be attacked, though the King '... consulted about how to decide in this important matter. He often warned and urged them to keep their mercenaries alarmed' — Rogerius says. Regarding the opinion of the court dignitaries. '... amidst the entertainment the Hungarians did not believe it (the news about the Mongol attack), and they kept repeating that they had already heard rumours about the Mongols, but they experienced that they had lacked any kind of reality. Others insisted that news like this was spread by some prelates because they did not want to go to the council where the Pope had invited them. Others — quite a few — kept explaining that they had good reasons to abuse the King as the Cumans had allied themselves with the Russians to fight against the Hungarians, who defeated and destroyed them several times. Kuthen (Kötöny) came with his people more than one year earlier to know the conditions of the country and to learn its language when informed about their arrival to start fighting against the King, so they can take possession of the Gate (the Pass of Verecke); and so they can destroy some parts of Hungary quicker. Thus they mischievously critisized the King for inviting the Cumans, as mentioned above. And a lot of them agreed with this opinion.'

The days passed in Óbuda full of such and similar emotions, while the Mongol armies were coming nearer and nearer. The dignitaries of the country who were against the Cumans managed to convince the King to order the Cuman King to come to Óbuda together with his family. From here they were taken to a house in Pest, where they were kept in custody; according to research the house may have been near the present Vigadó. By the middle of March the Mongol horde was reported to have succeeded in crossing the Pass of Verecke, and scattered the army of Palatine Denis, who tried to defend the country there. The King then finished the discussions and sent every prelate and landlord to their estates to recruit troops and meet later in Rákosmező. He sent his wife, Maria Laskaris and his children to the Austrian border to ask for defence and military help.

The rest of the story is quite well—known. Unfortunately the general feeling turned completely against the Cuman people when it was rumoured that there were Cumans fighting in the Mongol horde (it was not known that they must have been captured Cumans who were forced to fight); and the enraged crowd attacked the Kötöny's residence and massacred him and all his family. When hearing about this the Cumans left the country burning and plundering everything on their way. Near Muhi the Hungarian army had to face their fate without being prepared, not knowing the Mongol strategy.

In the winter of the following year Óbuda — including the royal mansion and St. Peter's provostry — was devastated, and it fell prey of the the troops of Khan Batu.

Chronology

c. 900   The conquering Hungarians cross the River Danube and occupy the territory of the present Óbuda.

902 or 904 The death of Prince Kurszan, Árpád exercises the power alone.

c. 907   The death of Prince Árpád The first part of the 11th century The foundation of the provostry consecrated to St. Peter

1148   The charter of King Géza II, in which he confirms the donations of King Ladislas I to the provostry

1196—c.1204 (Ó)buda is donated to the provost by King Emeric

1205   King Andrew II takes back King Emeric's donations

1212   (Ó)buda is donated to the provost by King Andrew II; the borders of the town are described The first third of the 13th century The second royal castle is built

1241—1242 Mongol invasion

1261   'Vetus Buda' — the name 'Óbuda' appears

1355   King Luis the Great divides Óbuda between the provost and the Queen

1526   Turkish attack

1541   Óbuda gets under Turkish rule for 150 years

Bibliography

Altmann, Julianna—Szirmai Krisztina: Előzetes jelentés a ferences templom és a Via Pretoriától északra húzódó rómaikori épületmaradványok régészeti kutatásáról (Preliminary Report about the archaelogical research of the Roman ruins from the Franciscan friary to Via Pretoria) BpR 24/I. 1976.

Altmann, Julianna: Újabb kutatások az óbudai királyi ill. királynéi vár területén (Latest research in the Óbuda castle of the kings, queens) BpR 24/I. 1976.

Altmann, Julianna: Neue Forschungen über die Burg der Königin In Óbuda (Latest research in the Óbuda castle of the Queen) ActaArchHung 34. 1982.

Altmann, Julianna: Ásatások a középkori Óbudán 1981—1991 között (Excavations in the medieval Óbuda between 1981 and 1991) BpR 29. 1992

Budapest Műemlékei (The monuments of Budapest) II. Bp. 1962.

Budapest Története (The History of Budapest) Ed. Gerevich, László. Bp. 1973.

Bártfai Szabó, László: Óbuda egyházi intézményei a középkorban (The ecclesiastical institutions of Óbuda in the Middle Ages) Bp. 1935.

Bertalan, Vilmosné: Adatok Óbuda középkori helyrajzához (Data to the medieval topography of Óbuda) Budapest Régiségei 23. 1973.

Bertalan, Vilmosné: Óbudai klarissza kolostor (The Convent of the Order of Poor Claire in Óbuda) BpR 24/I. 1976.

Bertalan, Vilmosné: A középkori óbudai ásatások 1850—1975. (The excavations of the medieval Óbuda 1850—1975) BpR 24/I. 1976.

Bertalan, Herta: Das Klarissenkloster von Óbuda aus dem XIV. Jahrhundert (The Convent of the Order of Poor Claire in Óbuda) Acta Archaelogica Hungarica 34. 1982.

Bertalan, Vilmosné: Óbuda — Vestus Buda — régészeti kutatások alapján (Óbuda — Vestus Buda — as archaelogical research shows) BpR 25. 1984.

Bertalan, Vilmosné: A Fő téren feltárt középkori maradványok (The medieval remains in Fő tér) BpR 25. 1984.

Bertalan, Vilmosné: Óbuda 1355-ös és 1437-es határjárásának régészetileg meghatározott határpontjai (The borders of Óbuda in 1355 and 1437 defined by archaelogical research) BpR 25. 1984.

Bertalan, Vilmosné: Középkori házak a budai káptalan területén (Medieval houses in the area of the Buda chapter) BpR 29. 1992.

Csemegi, József: Hol állott egykor az óbudai királyi vár? (Where was the Óbuda royal castle?) Magyar Mérnök- és Épitészegylet Közleményei 1943.

Csorba, Csaba: Az óbudai Szent Margit egyház és környékének kutatása (The archaelogical research of St Margaret's Church and its vicinity) BpR 24/I. 1976.

Fügedi, Elek: Topográfia és városi fejlődés a középkori Óbudán (Topography and the urban development in the medieval Óbuda) Tanulmányok Budapest Múltjából 13. 1959.

Garády, Sándor: Budapest székesfőváros területén végzett középkori ásatások összefoglaló ismertetése (The review of the excavations of the medieval Budapest) 1931—1941. BpR 13. 1943.

Győrffy, György: Kurszán és Kurszán vára (Kurszán and the castle of Kurszán) BpR 16. 1953.

Kumorovitz, Bernát L.: Isősb Erzsébet királyné épitkezéseinek történetéhez (About the history of the construction work of Queen Elizabeth) TBM 17. 1966.

Kumorovitz, Bernát L.: Buda (és Pest) "fővárossá" alakulásának kezdetei (The Beginning of the New Capital, Buda (and Pest)) TBM 18 1971.

Kumorovitz, Bernát L.: Óbuda 1355 évi felosztása (The division of Óbuda in 1355) BpR 24/I. 1976.

Lux, Kálmán: Árpád-kori épitészeti maradványok Óbudán (Árpádian remains in Óbuda) MMÉK 19. 1916.

SIGHTS

The sights of the royal seat can be seen in Óbuda and the archaelogical material is exhibited in the Budapest Historical Museum in the Budavári Palota (Buda palace).

1. Franciscan church and friary (Vöröskereszt utca, map: 3)
2. The remains of St. Mary's Church (Fő tér 1 and 6, map: 2)
3. Exhibition on the history of the town in the subway in Flórián tér

4. The portal leading into the chapel of the royal castle (Kálvin köz 2-4, map: 4)
5. The side chapel of St. Margaret's parish church (Templom utca, map: 7)
6. The medieval houses of the market place (Lajos utca 158. and its vicinity, map: 6)
7. The church and convent of the Order of Ploor Claire (Kiskorona utca — Perc utca, map: 8)

VISEGRÁD

Bonia
Lopна
Tanan
Ralonda
Werbil
Compes
Ludas
Erdetelet
Achie
Wenitz
Krupina
Mur
Toldtar
Rarayo
Bozoc
Nentisibitz
Palota
Cipel
Sohttam
Elck
Vispek
Pasach
Pata
Curt
Litwa
Bawal
S Jacob
Adlar
Arotzalos
Baras
Bvdoutz
Palastionis
Regel
Pongos
Josch
Tatwar
Jerenzam
Cegg
Bag Scigoly
Mores
Orol
Remie
Vihalon
Bartal
Tura
Rita
Pelou
Vift
Sirok
Chur
Ratala
Lena
Brick
Nenti
Wlad
Cipi
Cemet
Saibe
Fchalos
Berute
Vacia
Recega
Csar
Sayy
Tengeo
Rolta
Cgu
lota villa
Mares
Jrfojez
Pand
Ncrftur
Yler
Wyl
Danaw
Rebellut
Viftград
Anbr
Sobach
Warfan
Nayod
Strygoniu
flu Gran
Colfar
Ofen
Exel
Netel
Taxon
Romun
Labatlan
S Paulus
Eno
S Martinus
Donu
Afiuit
Loro
Meffon
Vygky
Centa colles
Ero
Tata
Erchi
Vyfahn
Banpida
Marton bafar
Cwertget
Befene
ov.vif
Vitan
Ciaal
Adom
Lell
Jenew
Bidnick
Fugetfch
Zenthiat
Stuel
Weifnburg
Palora
Vthida
Pentele
Rab
Taurinul
Labau
Eskew
Renest
S Marten perg
Monta

THE LANDSCAPE AND THE BEGINNING OF THE SETTLEMENT

Visegrád lies at the eastern gate of the Danube Bend, where the river breaks through the volcanic cliffs of the Börzsöny and Visegrád Hills, and arrives in a wide valley; then slowing down immediately starts to build the Szentendre Island. Over the Visegrád defile on the right bank a gradually widening plain is formed at the foot of the hills. The streams of the Visegrád Hills often formed heaps of alluvial deposit stretching deep into the river, which lended themselves to settlements free from floods and also facilitated crossing the river. There is a stream like this at the foot of Sibrik Hill, then in the centre of Visegrád the stream Apátkuti. Going upstream we arrive at the mouth of the stream Lepence.

On the left bank of the Danube the landscape is reverse. There, upstream the plain on the river bank gradually narrows; and at the peak of the bend, at Szent Mihály Hill it vanishes. This made the Visegrád ferry especially important, as the road from the eastern direction on the left bank had to cross the river here.

Archaelogical research has proved that this area has been populated since the copper age. Finds from the earliest peiod have been uncovered at the mouth of the stream Lepence. In the early iron age there was a fortified settlement on the castle hill.

This territory became especially important when the border of the Roman Empire reached the line of the Danube. Thus the Danube Bend was the stretch of the border which was the most often attacked by barbaric tribes so the best fortified by the Romans. In the 2nd and 3rd centuries it was enough to guard the border (limes) with watch—towers. In the first half of the 4th century, however, Constantin the Great and his descendants had to build a huge system of fortifications in the Danube Bend. One of the key points of this system was the Pone Navata castrum, which was built on top of Sibrik Hill, with its steep side rising over the river, and besides it there were several watch—towers and a small fort in the territory of the present—day settlement.

At the beginning of the 5th century, as the empire was declining, there was no money for the maintenance of the fortresses. The soldiers who were mainly of barbaric origin tried to maintain the fortresses with smaller, improper repairs. Soon, however, when the Huns appeared, this situation became hopeless, and the Romans surrendered Pannonia. The decayed fortresses on the borderline soon became ruins, and nobody settled there.

After this in the territory of Visegrád there was a more important settlement only in the Avar period, but it started to flourish only at the time of the foundation of the Hungarian state.

The 10th—12th Centuries

After the Hungarian conquest the huge woodland of the Pilis Hills was in the property of Árpád's descendants. The centre of this hunting—field was Visegrád. The ruined Roman fortress was repaired; and St Stephen made it a bailiff seat. The county of Visegrád — as the foundation document of the Veszprém bishopric proves — existed already in 1002. The bailiff castle built from the Roman fortress, which the Slavs living in the vicinity called Visegrád, i.e. 'higher castle', lay where the main road on the Danube bank was forced among the hills to avoid the hill of the castle on the bank of the river. In the small valley of a stream, where the road led up to the castle, some settlements of scattered houses developed. Beside the mouth of the stream, on the bank of the Danube was one of the villages, among its houses half dug into the earth several workshops, e.g. a non—ferrous metal melting furnace came to light. This shows that the inhabitants of the village were mostly craftsmen who worked for the bailiff castle. Beside the castle the earliest parish church of Visegrád was built still around 1000. It was a small, one—aisled church with a semicircular chancel.

Visegrád played a special role during the reign of King Andrew I and his son, King Solomon. These two severeigns must often have visited the castle in the middle of the hunting—field. Andrew I founded a Greek orthodox Basilite monostary consecrated to St Andrew at the edge of the settlement; and most probably King Solomon built a much bigger and richer church in the place of the small parish church beside the castle. On the settlement near the Danube a small church was built also then. At this time a big stone palace, divided into two rooms on the goundfloor, was erected in the bailiff castle. This residential building, which was unusual in bailiffs' castles, must have met not only the needs of the bailiff but also those of the king, who from time to time came here. When St Ladilas dethroned Solomon, he sent him into exile in his own castle in Visegrád, where Solomon was kept in custody till 1083, when he was set free on the occasion of King Stephen's canonization.

St Ladislas just like his father, Béla I used the Dömös mansion; so during their reign Visegrád lost its importance, which it did not regain in the 12th century. In 1242 the Mongol invasion ruined the settlement together with the castle, the churches and St Andrew's monastery, which in the meantime got in the hands of the Benedictines.

Visegrád after the Mongol Invasion

After the Mongol invasion a new phase started in the history of Visegrád. In 1249 Queen Mary, the wife of Béla IV, probably afraid of another Mongol invasion started to build a new castle on the price of her own jewellery on the rocky hilltop above the old Visegrád. As a charter later says she built this castle for the Dominican nuns on the Island of Rabbits (the present—day Margaret

Island) to be able to find refuge from the Mongols if necessary. The upper castle must have been finished by 1251. The danger of another Mongol invasion was already over, but the construction work was continued: a wall between the upper castle and the Danube, fortified with towers and closing the valley was built. Beside the road leading through it, an enormous hexagonal donjon was erected which is falsely called today 'Salamon's tower (Solomon's) to commemorate King Solomon, who was kept in custody in Visegrád in the 11th century. The castle now served not only as a refuge castle but it was also the residential place of the bailiffs of the county of Pilis, when hunting the king stayed here as well. In 1265 Béla IV spent the hunting season here.

Not only the castle had a new place but the settlement revived in a new place as well: south of the lower castle, at the foot of the castle hill on the plain along the Danube. The centre of the settlement developed at the junction of the ferry at the mouth of the stream Apátkút, the road leading to the castle and the main road on the bank of the Danube, in the place of a village most probably existing already before the Mongol invasion. The inhabitants were privileged settlers (hospes).

VISEGRÁD AND THE ANGEVIN PERIOD

After the death of King Andrew III in 1301 the castle was most probably occupied by the Czech soldiers of King Wenceslas. Then it was in the hand of Máté Csák, who was able to prevent that Charles Robert of the House of Anjou ruled over the middle of the country as well. Máté Csák, who was at war with the Czech king, was attacked by Charles Robert, whose supporters occupied the Komárom castle, then in a long siege the Visegrád castle as well.

Charles Robert, however, only decided to move his seat from the distant Temesvár to the middle of the country after the Máté Csák's death, in 1323. He chose Visegrád, where the strongest castle of the middle of the country was to be found and not Buda, which was big and rich but not so safe.

Charles Robert first wanted to make the castle stronger and habitable for the court. The construction work must have been quite fast: in 1325 the church of St John, the Baptist was already standing in the castle. This can be identified with one of the vaulted rooms on the fifth level of the donjon of the lower castle.

In the upper castle, where the royal regalia were guarded since 1323, there was significant building work going on as well. This cannot be dated, but it is probable that by the end of the 1370s in the inner castle three palace wings were erected, the second circle wall was built together with the lower bailey. This work was done in several stages.

The nearness of the court advanced the development of the settlement under the castle as well, and it soon became an important town. In the middle of the 14th century Visegrád consisted of two parts. The bigger and more important was the Hungarian town, where the parish church consecrated to St Mary was situated. This settlement must have been near the ferry. Much less is known about the German town. It was probably of less importance, though it was represented in the town council with six members just like the Hungarian town. There is no data about any ramparts. A big gate was only mentioned once in the German town, but it may have been the gate of the lower castle where the main road went through. In both parts of the town there were houses, mansions and towers built of wood and stone.

Charles Robert built his mansion, in the Hungarian part of the town, which was close to the German town. It was first mentioned in the Illuminated Chronicle as it was the scene of Felician Zách' infamous assasin attempt in 1330.

Several remains of significant buildings are known from this period on the territory of the later palace. Some of them must have belonged to the royal mansion, but it is not possible yet to identify them. Around 1340 new construction work started on this territory, a church was begun but the work was soon stopped. This was perhaps caused by the political changes in the 1340s. In 1342 Charles Robert died in the upper castle. During the first part of the reign of his son, Luis I (the Great), between 1347 and 1355, the royal court was in Buda. The rebuilding and enlarging of the Visegrád palace was only started when the court moved back.

The building of the chamber in the town was already mentioned in 1356. The accomplishment of the work is indicated by the 1366 papal permit of indulgence given to St Mary's Chapel built in the royal palace. The area of the palace was somewhat bigger than its is today. The palace built in the second third of the 14th century was a conglomerate of buildings with different functions, built in several stages. The type of building putting the residential buildings, chapel, chamber and service buildings beside each other, lacking any real fortification was a well—known form of royal residence all over Europe in the 13th—14th centuries. The royal palace on the Cité Island in Paris, the palace in Westminster near London or in Central Europe the mansion of the Czech kings in the old town in Prague and their chamber in Kutnahora represented this type of building. The other residential place of the Hungarian kings of the House of Anjou, Magna Curia, also known as Kammerhof in Buda had the same arrangement.

VISEGRÁD IN THE AGE OF SIGISMUND

The last third of the 14th and the first third of the 15th century brought about a golden age for arts all over Europe: the international Gothic style spread from the royal courts. As the political emphasis was gradually shifted towards the east — during the reign of Charles IV and Wenceslas IV to Prague then in the age of Sigismund to Buda — the ideals of arts born in France and Italy also found good grounds here in the first half of the 14th century; moreover in the second half of the 14th century this area was as significant a birthplace of late Gothic as Western Europe. In the birth of the late Gothic art in Hungary the construction in Visegrád at the end of the 14th century played a leading role. When the royal court moved to Buda in the second half of this period the significance of Visegrád decreased though, the results of the Gothic art developing in Buda had influence here as well. These decades can rightly be considered the golden age of Visegrád. The most important royal and ecclesiastical buildings were built in this period. Later they were only modified, embellished or just reconstructed. From architectural point of view Visegrád became a classical medieval town and a royal residence around 1400.

The most significant building of this period was the new royal palace. Luis I and Elizabeth started the enlargement of the old palace at the end of the 1370s; but after their death their daughter, Queen Mary and after 1387 her husband Sigismund created a completely new, much more luxurious building complex than the one planned originally.

The palace with its regular ground—plan, splendid fountains and demanding execution was an outstanding piece of art of the European architecture around 1400. The patterns of its regular ground—plan were the Palace of the Popes in Avignon as well as the castles of Diósgyőr and Zólyom, which were typical representatives of the Hungarian architecture in the last third of the 14th century. The details showed Bohemian influence.

King Sigismund had construction work going on in the upper castle as well: the outer curtain wall and a new palace wing in the inner castle were built in the first third of the 15th century.

In the time of Sigismund the most important buildings of the town were rebuilt as well. St Mary's parish church was vaulted by the builders of the palace chapel. The stone carvings of another church excavated only partly also suggest significant building work around 1400. This may have been the church of the Augustinian friary mentioned only in one source.

Visegrád remained the capital till about 1405—1408, when the royal court moved to Buda, where Sigismund started to build huge palaces. Visegrád, however, remained the favourite residential place of the king, and there were new buildings erected as well. The most important of these was the Observant Franciscan friary. When the palace was constructed, the older St George's palace chapel got outside the building complex, thus it lost its importance. King Sigismund bestowed the chapel on the Observant Franciscan order invited from Bosnia, and also built a house for them beside it. This is known from the charter written in 1424, in which the Pope confirms the privileges of the Visegrád Franciscans. The charter was written as the King was planning to enlarge the chapel into a church 'with a belfry, bells, a cloister, a churchyard and other necessary workshops and appropriate buildings'. The King seems to have changed his mind, as he did not enlarge St George's palace chapel — it is mentioned as a deserted building in sources from the Jagellonian period — but built a new friary and a church consecrated to St Mary after 1425.

THE DECAY OF VISEGRÁD IN THE MIDDLE OF THE 15TH CENTURY

Visegrád was quickly declining in the 1440s. One of the ladies—in—waiting of Queen Elizabeth, Mrs Helena Kottanner stole the crown for the child Ladislas V from the upper castle in 1440; only King Matthias was able to buy it back from Emperor Frederick III in 1463. The kings spent less and less time in the palace; moreover King Matthias bestowed the Visegrád estate on his first wife Catherine of Podebrad in 1461; it got back to the possession of the King after her death in 1464.

VISEGRÁD IN THE AGE OF KING MATTHIAS

King Matthias only turned his attention to Visegrád in the 1470s. In 1474 he invited settlers to revive the town, and after 1476 he started to rebuild the palace. To facilitate this he placed the Visegrád royal estate also under the authority of the court marshal in Buda, who organized the construction work.

Now the palace was only built to be a country residence, magnificant though, and not a royal seat as a hundred years ago.

The construction was started with the representative palace wings of the lower reception court between 1476 and 1481, the north—eastern palace was rebuilt around 1484, and the work was finished before 1490.

The century—old buildings of the Visegrád palace were renewed and modernized from the floors to the roof, the fountains and stoves changed. The renewal was spectacular, though there were hardly any new buildings built, almost every door and window frame, fireplace, pillar was replaced with late Gothic ones.

The building work can basically be characterized with late Gothic style. The taste of the Italian Renaissance is only reflected in sculptural work and smaller architectural work like fountains, the furnishings of the chapel and the loggia of the ceremonial court of the north—eastern palace.

Some members of the building workshop participating in the reconstruction of the palace also worked on the rebuilding of the upper castle in the time of King Matthias. The inner courtyard was enclosed with palaces then. The lower and upper castles were fortified to a smaller extent in this period as well.

VISEGRÁD AT THE END OF THE MIDDLE AGES

After the death of King Matthias, in 1492 Parliament decided that the upper castle should be under the authority of the guards of the crown, as probably it had already been the place where the crown was kept since the time of Charles Robert. The lower castle and the palace remained in the hand of the king. The palace was the favourite place of residence of the kings of the House of Jagello; and King John of Szapolya also spent a longer period of time here with his wife Isabel in 1539. The buildings, which were already quite dilapidated, were renewed and tidied for the occasion.

THE DECAY OF THE MEDIEVAL VISEGRÁD

In the following years civil strife and from 1544 the Turkish occupation determined the fate of Visegrád. In the fights the palace was burned, its walls started to decay. In a Turkish siege in 1544 the southern corner of the donjon of the lower castle collapsed burying the south—western corner of the inner castle as well. After the siege a small Turkish settlement developed among the remaining walls. The upper castle was also damaged in the sieges; in the 16th—17th centuries it was not rebuilt only slightly repaired. Finally, in 1685 the Turkish troops left and set the building on fire, blew up the defence system; thus the castle was ruined.

In the 18th century after the Turks were driven out, the new owners of Visegrád and the new settlers of the village used the ruins of the palace and the town as a quarry, so in one and a half centuries the one—time grand buildings completely disappeared.

Archaelogical research and reconstruction started in the castle in 1871, in the palace in 1934, and they have been going on ever since.

THE UPPER CASTLE IN VISEGRÁD

THE VIEW OF VISEGRÁD *from W. Dillich's work 'Vngarische Cronica...' published in 1600.*
The etching depicts the castle and the town still undamaged, though earlier trustworthy etchings from 1595 already show ruins. It is also known from written sources that the Christian siege in 1595 caused the biggest damage; moreover some parts of the castle were ruined already in 1544 when the Turks shelled the southern part of the donjon in the lower castle. Dillich's etching, however, shows an undamaged castle, the reason for which must be that an earlier drawing made maybe still before the Turkish times was copied, and it was made updated with some minarets.

THE VIEW OF VISEGRÁD, *etching based on the drawing of Jakob Hoefnagel in 1595.*
In the siege in 1595 the Visegrád castle was completely ruined. The view in Hoefnagel's drawing hardly differs from the sight today. The towers and palace wings of the upper castle collapsed, the walls only remained intact on the more-protected Danube side. The donjon of the lower castle had been in ruins with its collapsed corner for a long time, just like the town and the palace, which was overgrown with woods and bushes by the end of the 16th century. Among the walls of the lower castle the houses of a small Turkish settlement were to be found.

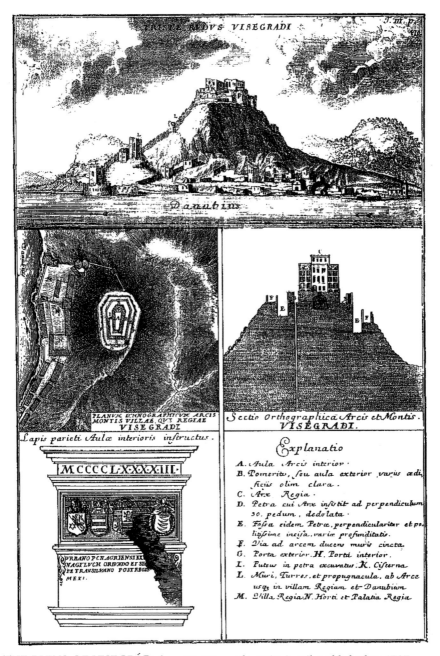

THE RUINS OF VISEGRÁD *from 'Notitia ...' by Mátyás Bél, published in 1737.* The etching still shows tall walls in the place of the palace. The ruins of the palace were mostly standing till the middle of the 18th century when conscious destruction started.

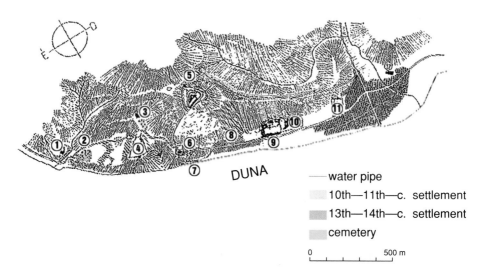

DUNA

——— water pipe

10th—11th—c. settlement

13th—14th—c. settlement

cemetery

0   500 m

THE MEDIEVAL TOPOGRAPHY OF VISEGRÁD

1. St Andrew's monastery; 2. 10th—12th—c. settlement and church; 3. 11th—12th—c. parish church; 4. 4th—c. Roman fortress, 10th—12th—c. bailiff castle; 5. Upper castle, 13th—16th c; 6. Lower castle with donjon; 7. Port; 8. German town; 9. Royal palace; 10. St Mary's Franciscan friary; 11. Augustinian church, 14th—15th c; 12. St Mary's parish church; 13. Hungarian town; 14. Ferry to Nagymaros

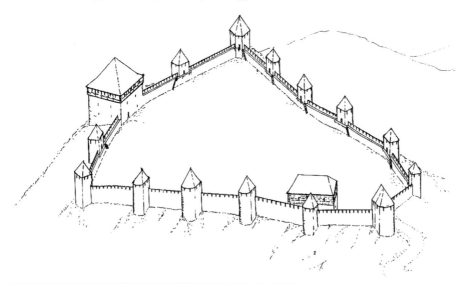

THE RECONSTRUCTION OF THE BAILIFF CASTLE

The Roman fortress of Pone Navata was built in the 4th c. It had an irregular ground—plan, its walls were fortified with horseshoe— and fan–shaped towers, the buildings were erected along the walls. The gate surrounded with towers opened in the middle of the most protected side towards the Danube. In the place of this gate a big

but thin walled tower was built still during the Roman period at the end of the 4th or at
the beginning of the 5th c. After the Romans left Pannonia the fortress was uninhabited.
Though the walls were not repaired for about six hundred years, at the end of the 10th
c. they were in so good condition that King St Stephen — or perhaps Prince Géza —
considered the fortress worth rebuilding in an unchanged form. Besides Visegrád there
were other castles as well which were rebuilt on the Roman walls, e.g. Gyulafehérvár,
Sopron and Győr, but in the latter two timber structured entrenchment was also built
behind the remains of the Roman walls. The stone palace of the bailiff, with two big
rooms, maybe with an upper floor, was built in the north—eastern side of the castle
after the reconstruction of the castle but still in the 11th c. The bailiff castle was
destroyed by Mongols in 1242. Its ruins were used in the building of the new Visegrád
castle in the following decades.

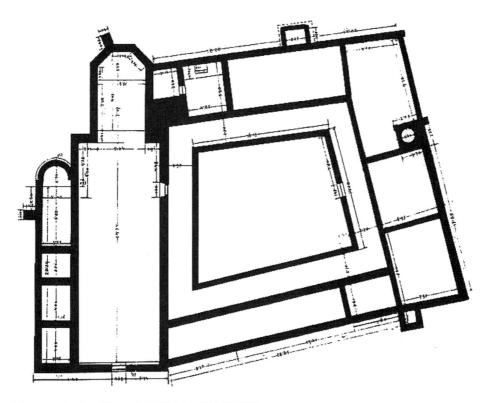

THE PLAN OF ST ANDREW'S MONASTERY

The Basilite monastery founded by Andrew I was given to the Benedictine Order by Pope Honorius III in 1221. In 1242 the Mongols destroyed it together with the whole settlement. Béla IV may have considered the reconstruction when the new Visegrád castle was built, so in 1257 he confirmed the donation of St Ladislas. It was, however, reconstructed much later, in the time of Charles Robert. We have data about the work from 1333, and in 1342 the provincial chapter of the Order was held in the rebuilt monastery. Only the northern aisle of the three—aisled Romanesque church was left; in the place of the nave and the southern aisle a new, wide nave was built, which was closed with a long poligonal chancel. The whole church was covered with cross—ribbed vaulting. When in 1386 an attempt was made on Charles II's life in Buda, the seriously injured sovereign was brought to Visegrád, where he died; but as he was excommunicated, it was not possible to bury him properly. His body was put into earth in the territory of St Andrew's monastery, and when the papal permission arrived in 1391, he was buried here, too. By the end of the 15th c. the monastery was almost uninhabited: for years only one monk lived there. So in 1493 Pope Alexander VI through the good offices of Tamás Bakócz, Bishop of Eger, the monastery was taken from the Benedictines and given to the Paulines. Bakócz helped with a donation of 50 golden forints to reconstruct the neglected and ruined building. The big square late Gothic cloister was built at this time. The passageways were covered with cross—ribbed vaulting. The tower in the southern part of the chancel and the nave was probably erected by the Paulines, too. In the newly rebuilt monastery the nephew of the King, Sigismund Polish prince spent a longer period of time in the summer of 1500. The building was left by the Paulines probably after the Turkish occupation in 1544. Its ruins were excavated by Béla Czobor in 1890 and 1894 but a villa was built in its place in the 1920s.

11TH CENTURY CUSHION CAPITAL *from St Andrew's monastery*

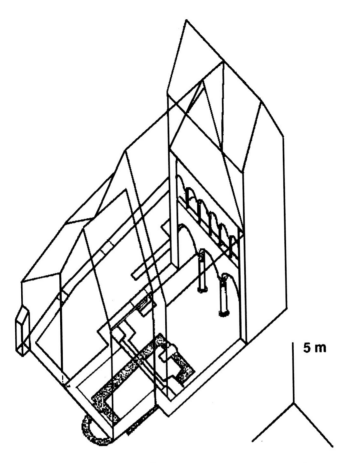

THE PARISH CHURCH IN VISEGRÁD, MID 11TH C, *reconstuction*
The first small church built around 1000 had a rectangular nave and a semicircular chancel. In the middle of the 11th century, probably in the time of King Solomon, it was pulled down, and a much bigger, richly ornamented church with a more complicated arrangement was built in its place. Its chancel had a square ground—plan, in the rectangular nave there were two side altars. The nave was divided into two with a wooden roodscreen in the middle, and in its western end a gallery was built richly ornamented with stone carvings. The gallery probably with a wide tower above it was accessible on a staircase built outside the southern side of the nave. An outer passage was also added to this side. The inside of the church was ornamented with frescoes. The parishes in the county centre always played a more important role than the others in the county, so they were more and more often called archdioceses. The parish church beside the Visegrád castle also became an archdeaconry see, but it soon began to decline: the church was abandoned before the Mongol invasion, perhaps already in the 12th c; the archdeacon is proved to have resided in Szentendre at the beginning of the 13th c.

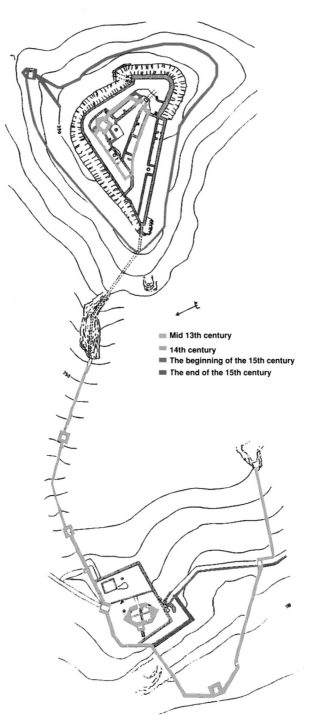

Mid 13th century
14th century
The beginning of the 15th century
The end of the 15th century

THE PERIODS OF THE CASTLE, PLAN

The main plan of the Visegrád castle was already formed in the middle of the 13th century. The upper castle was erected on the top of the hill. The gatehouse was in the southern corner of the more or less triangular ramparts. A pentagonal donjon was built in the eastern corner most exposed to attacks. The residential building was probably in the most protected western corner, probably of wood as excavations have not found any sign of it. The cictern beside the palace, however, can still be seen.

There was a curtain wall between the upper castle and the Danube. A stretch of cliff served as the upper part of the rampart, the built wall only began at its foot. The upper section of the rampart was passable only in some parts, so the two watchtowers here were only accessible — at least in peaceful times — on a path outside the wall through small doors.

Where the road crossed the rampart a strong gatehouse was built. The big donjon of the castle was erected behind the gatehouse. The lower section of the rampart below the gatehouse was passable. There was another watchtower at the bank of the Danube. This ensured the water supply of the castle and at the same time protected the nearby port. Another wall ran upwards to the south of the tower. The road crossed this wall through a simple gate only protected with a protruding wall. The southern rampart did not go as high up as the northern, only up to the point where the hillside rose steeply.

Around the donjon of the lower castle Charles Robert built an inner, square curtain wall on the higher, eastern side of which an enclosed terrace was constructed. The well of the castle and a minting chamber were here, too. A bridge led from here to the entrance protected with a drawbridge on the third level of the donjon. The inside of the donjon was significantly rebuilt as well. The ground floor was divided into four rooms with crossing walls, the second level into two with a north—south oriented wall and the other levels into two as well most probably with east—west oriented walls. The wooden ceiling of the fifth level was replaced with ribbed vaulting.

The Angevin period rebuilding of the upper castle was accomplished in several steps. In the inner castle the biggest eastern palace with a large hall on each level was finished first, perhaps still in the time of Charles Robert. This two—level wing adjusted to the original surface of the steeply rising inner bailey. Outside the donjon a second cictern was cut and walled with bricks. Later the level of the inner bailey was made horizontal and the original height of the cliff was only left around the two cistern. The western palace wing was built then as well. A kitchen was on the ground floor. On the first floor a heated, wooden—panelled room and a hall lit with big windows, separated with a wooden wall were situated. The second floor of the palace wing with only one huge hall was erected later. After the level of the courtyard was lowered certainly in the second half of the 14th century, the northern palace wing was built in the place of the supposed 13th—century one in the north—western corner of the castle, adjusted to the cliff left around the old cistern. On the ground floor one, on the first floor three rooms were situated. The outer rampart was divided into two sections. In the more protected western side a wide farmyard was to be found with another cistern. The northern and eastern sides were encircled with a narrow defile of walls, which enlarged into a wide bastion outside the gatehouse in the southern part. The wooden bridge crossing the moat was here, too. The moat cut into the rocks which were used in the building of the ramparts encircled the castle on the northern, eastern, southern and south—western sides. It not only protected the castle but probably also contained farm buildings, stables as well, as the inner courtyards were not accessible for carts and horses.

The outer rampart, which was a thin and low parapeted counterfort, was built in the first third of the 15th century, in the time of Sigismund. The only fortified part was the pentagonal eastern gatehouse which was adjacent to the moat of the middle castle with a Y—shaped wall.

The ladies' house in the territory of the inner castle, between the northern palace wing and the donjon, with a wooden covered cellar cut into the cliff, must have been built then as well.

Here a grand hall and a staircase were constructed between the western and northern wings, and the lane between the eastern palace wing and the donjon was also built in at the age of Matthias. The old buldings were completely converted. All the cellars and the ground—floor rooms were rebuilt with bricked barrel vaulting; the ground—floor levels of the eastern and western wings were considerably lowered. The first level of the western wing was covered with a beamed ceiling on stone supports, that of the eastern wing with net vaulting. The windows were replaced with late Gothic mullioned windows of different sizes.

In the lower courtyard the lean—to roofed farm building was erected, the room south of the cistern was covered with barrel vaulting. Because of this the rampart around the courtyard was considerably heightened. The section of the defile in the middle castle, which was close to the donjon and most exposed to shelling was filled up; and to protect the entrance to the inner castle a small bastion was built to the east of the gate.

In the lower castle the cistern beside the donjon must have been dug after the Angevin period well had been filled up; and the terrace with cannons, encircling the western side and south—western corner of the inner castle, may have been built then as well.

THE FORTIFICATION SYSTEM IN THE 13TH CENTURY, *reconstruction* ≫→

The fortification system consisting of an upper castle, a wall closing the valley and a donjon had two functions. On the one hand, as a county centre and a royal 'hunting—seat' it was a representative residential place; on the other, it ensured the control of the waterway of the Danube and the road on the river bank.

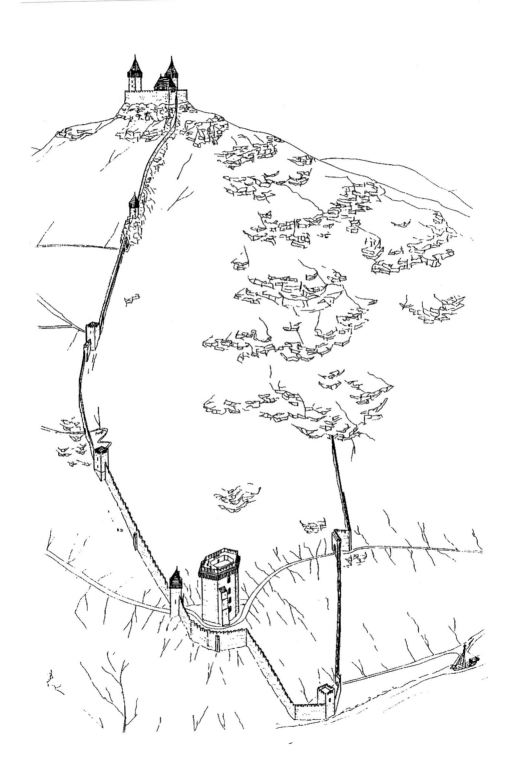

THE 13TH—CENTURY DONJON OF THE LOWER CASTLE

The huge, hexagonal donjon served both as a fortress and a representative residential building. There were big, stretched octagonal—shaped halls on each of the five lower levels. Their beamed ceilings were supported with three pillars. The ground floor had a separate entrance. Its loop—holes ensured that the road around the tower was protected. The upper levers were accessible through the door on the first floor. The first—, second—, third— and fourth—floor rooms lit with two ornamented coupled windows and heated with big fireplaces were reached through a wide spiral staircase built in the southern corner. A toilet belonged to each level, which according to the original plan were to have been built in the thick wall; but the plan was changed and a turret was built for the toilets on the western side. An open terrace was situated on the sixth level, where different catapults and spear—throwing war engines were placed during battles to defend against the batteries of the besiegers on Sibrik Hill. Stairs led up to the battlement of the crowning with loop—holes for archers. Two doors led from the terrace to the wooden—structured machicolated gallery running round the tower, the defenders were able to shield the walls from the enemy already reaching the foot of the tower.

THE 13TH—CENTURY GATEHOUSE OF THE UPPER CASTLE

THE YARD OF THE INNER CASTLE

THE UPPER CASTLE IN THE 1370s, *reconstruction*

THE UPPER CASTLE IN THE TIME OF SIGISMUND, *reconstruction*

THE UPPER CASTLE IN THE TIME OF MATTHIAS, *reconstruction*

KEYSTONE WITH THE COAT OF ARMS OF QUEEN BEATRIX
from the grand hall of the upper castle

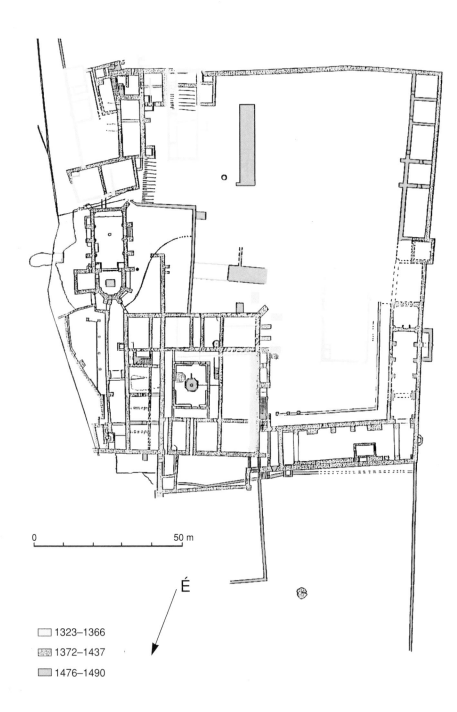

0 ————————— 50 m

É

☐ 1323–1366

▨ 1372–1437

☐ 1476–1490

THE ARCHITECTURAL PERIODS OF THE ROYAL PALACE

The remains of the oldest buildings found in the territory of the palace are dated at the 1320s—1330s. Two relatively small two—level stone buildings stood on the southern hillside, and a wooden house on the other terrace of the hillside. To the north of them a more or less square courtyard was formed by the encircling walls on the terrace cut into the hillside. In the courtyard there certainly were buildings as well, but they were destroyed during the later construction work. In front of it a huge, a two—level stone house was built in the territory of the present—day reception court, around 1340 a stone carving workshop moved here. A new building was built on the southern side of the mansion in the hillside. The highly ornamented stones of the chancel of a chapel were carved during the construction of this building, but they were never put into their place. The building of the church, however, was stopped; and the finished or half—finished carvings were walled up in the foundation of three huge buttresses probably after 1355 when the building of the stone carving workshop was pulled down. These buttresses were built in front of the western facade of the new southern wing, probably as part of the representative entrance. The chamber house was built then at the southern part of the palace, near the above—mentioned Charles Robert period buildings at the foot of the hill. The 13 m x 32 m building was cut into the hillside. Its cellar was built of stones and divided into two. The upper level was timber structured, probably with wooden covering. A stone counterfort protected it from the pressure of the hillside. The counterfort has left the impression of the beam structure of the wall. This level was also divided into two; in the southern room a foundry was to be found. When the chamber house was built, the earlier wooden house standing beside it was rebuilt as well.

The new palace built at the end of the 14th century occupied a territory of 123 m x 123 m. Its entrance was in the gatehouse in the axis of Danube side. The large reception court was situated on the plain area between the road and the slope of the castle hill. On the north side it was closed by a building with a 38.5 m x 11 m grand hall with a wooden vaulting, which was adjacent to a wing with representative rooms, parallel with the road on the west and to a quadrangular residential palace on the east. The most important parts of the north—eastern residential palace, a 11 m x 22 m grand hall on the ground floor and the first floor, were situated in the western wing overlooking the reception court. Ornamented stairs led to the ground—floor hall directly from the court; the first—floor hall was accessible through a spiral staircase. The inner courtyard of the north—eastern palace was decorated with a arcaded gallery on octagonal pillars, with niches and probably with an open corridor on the first floor. The main ornamentation of the yard, a monumental, octagonal fountain joined the arcades. The residential halls must have been on the first floor with a toilet tower on the north. The bathroom with floor—heating, a boiler and cold running water, was accessible across a bridge from the second floor. From this floor another bridge led to a small enclosed yard which was ornamented with a splendid fountain. In the western side of the yard there was a colonnade with niches. From the southern end of the colonnade a further bridge led to the royal oratory, which was the first floor room of the sacristy of the chapel. The huge chapel was built in the axis of the building complex, opposite the gatehouse, on a terrace cut into the hillside. The southern palace wing was less regular in shape because some rooms of the royal mansion were reused, too. On the uppermost level, the multi—storey buildings of much poorer quality surrounded a small, more or less square yard. In front of the western rooms a terrace was formed on a lower level, the rooms of the mint opened from here.

In the time of Matthias the main facade of the palace looking onto the Danube was built in and embellished with a huge bay window ornamented with coats of arms. The courtyards of the palace were also changed, the northern side of the first reception court was encircled with a two—level late Gothic colonnade. In front of the chapel a new terrace was built with large—sized ornamental stairs. In the inner yard of the north—eastern palace a two—level cloister walk was built — late Gothic on the ground floor and Renaissance on the first floor. In the middle of the court the octagonal Gothic fountain was replaced with the red marble Hercules—fountain. The rooms around the court were also rebuilt, and the second floor was completely built then as well. Here lower rooms with wooden ceilings, the king's residential rooms were situated with the considerably enlarged bathroom.

In the small yard the old colonnade and the fountain were replaced as well, in the place of the latter a red marble late Gothic fountain was carved ornamented with lions and coats of arms, on its canopy the raven in the coat of arms of the Hunyadi family and 1483, the year when the fountaim was made are to be seen.

The place of the red marble fountain ornamented with the Muses and known from Miklós Oláh's description has not been detected.

Only small—scale work was done in the palace chapel: white marble Renaissance alters, tabernacle and an organ embellished with silver pipes were put in. The organ loft was supported with with Renaissance consoles ornamented with coats of arms. In the southern end of the nave a wooden choir was erected which joined to the grand hall of the southern palace with a bridge. The sacristy and the royal oratory above it were vaulted. The floor and the roof of the chapel were covered with coloured, glazed tiles.

There were changes in the southern palace as well: the big hall in the north wing of the upper court was shaped from two smaller rooms, in one of its corners a huge but simple fireplace was put in. The old buildings over the southern wall of the palace complex were pulled down, and the small airshaft on the lower level was built in. The southern palace remained less important in the time of Matthias as well.

THE RECONSTRUCTED LOWER LEVEL OF THE 14TH CENTURY FOUNTAIN OF THE CEREMONIAL COURT

The inner court of the residential building of the palace was decorated with an open arcaded gallery which was adjacent to this magnificient fountain. Originally the fountain had two levels so it was accessible from the upper level of the gallery. As it was topped with a pinnacle, it looked like a tower. Similar, splendid works only remained in contemporary descriptions (like in the miniature of the Limburg brothers, depicting the paradise in the hour book, Trés Riches Heures, made for Prince Berry at the beginning of the 15th century) and in models of goldsmith's works (like a centre piece made in Paris around 1400, now kept in Cleveland). The model of the fountain may have been somewhere in France, maybe in Paris; but while it cannot be detected, the fountain in Visegrád can be reconstructed. It was also pulled down at the end of the 15th c. but its stones were used in the walls and the foundation of the new fountain. This made it possible for the excellent sculptor—conservator, Ernő Szakál to build a reconstruction standing now in the Salamon tower in Visegrád.

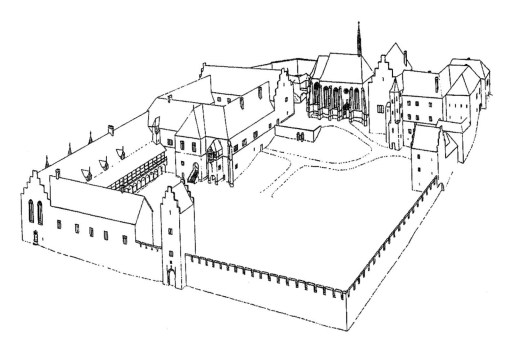

THE PALACE, SIGISMUND PERIOD, *reconstruction*

Tile stoves appeared in Hungary at the end of the 14th c. This kind of heating was first used in Switzerland in the 14th c. Tile stoves are ovens consisting of patterned, often glazed tiles plastered together. In the Angevin period they were quite rare in Hungary, but by the beginning of the 15th c. they were commonly used. The Visegrád palace was decorated with big ornamental stoves since the age of Luis the Great. The stove in the picture was made in the Sigismund period, at the beginning of the 15th c. Its tiles are ornamented with the coats of arms of the king, scenes from tales, castles, leaves and tracery. The rooms of the palace were heated with many similar stoves sometimes of different types of tiles. These stoves imitated the shape of Gothic towers. All of them were multicoloured thus fitting into the colourful picture of the Gothic palace ornamented with tapestry, painted stone and wood carvings.

TILE STOVE FROM THE VISEGRÁD PALACE, SIGISMUND PERIOD

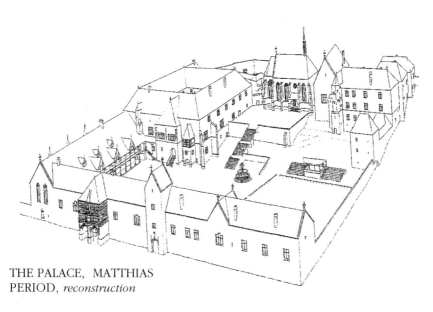

THE PALACE, MATTHIAS PERIOD, *reconstruction*

THE NORTH—EASTERN PALACE, PERSPECTIVE RECONSTRUCTION

The residential building of the palace complex, i.e. the north—eastern palace was considerably altered in the time of Matthias. From the 14th—c. building almost only the main walls were left, in some rooms even the partitions were changed. The most significant modification, however, was the two—level gallery in the court. On the ground floor a late Gothic cloister walk was built with big lancet glazed windows, some ornamented doors and star vaulting inside. The builders carved in the date of the construction, 1484, onto one of the ribs. On the first floor a Renaissance loggia was erected with a balustrade of red marble balusters, above them Renaissance pillars for the brick arches to support the flat ceiling. This loggia is the only Renaissance architectural srtucture in the palace, but it represented the most modern trends: this was the first Renaissance pillared arcade with balustrade which encircled a whole courtyard. This element originating in Visegrád became one of the favourite structures of Renaissance architecture in the following centuries. This also proves that Matthias' court played an outstanding role in the development of Renaissance art, but it has to be emphasized that the Renaissance and late Gothic elements and stuctures appear together on the loggia just like on the whole Visegrád palace. The two different styles harmonize here as well as in the contemporary Venice, Lombardy or Dalmatia, in the other outlying areas of the Italian Renaissance.

THE RECONSTRUCTED EASTERN CLOISTER WING

THE HERCULES FOUNTAIN, *reconstruction*

The Renaissance fountain was carved when the late Gothic cloister and the Renaissance loggia were built in the Matthias period c. 1484. Above the two—steps of the base, the side plates of the octagonal basin were carved of red marble, three complete and one fragmented have remained. The plates were decorated with a cornice and volutes on the top, the sides with simple framed mirrors, on them different crests encircled with festoons. All the coats of arms refer to King Matthias: the raven of the House of Hunyadi, the quartered Hungarian and Czech royal coat of arms with a raven of the House of Hunyadi in the heart—shield, the double—tailed lion of Bohemia and the coat of arms of the Beszterce Counts acquired by János Hunyadi, with its rearing lion holding a crown. As the arthistorian, Mária Réti's latest investigations prove the side plates were carved by a number of stone carvers. The simpler parts and festoons must have been made by the assistants of the workshop. The coats of arms, however, were definitely carved by the same person, a highly talented sculptor who may also have designed the fountain. The work on the other parts of the fountain was shared in the same way: the figural details were more consistent and higher standard than the simpler parts and the foliage. The central pillar was divided with three pilaster strips with a putto on each. The putti held the huge round platter from which the water ran through spouts into the corners of the basin. The bottom of the platter was embellished with exquisite geometrical ornaments. Three ram's head spouts were on the side of the richly decorated round base of the statue in the middle of the platter. The statue depicted Hercules dressed in lion skin, fighting with the hydra. Strangely enough the mythological hero is represented as a child. The statue, which has a complicated structure and was carved with excellent skills, is an outstanding piece of the 15th—c. Renaissance art. The sculptor may have made other works as well the Visegrád palace.

Besides its high artistic value the Hercules Fountain is of great significance as it is the only specimen that has remained in its original form. Though this type was to be found in large numbers in Italy in the second half of the 15th century, they were pulled down later; so they are only known from contemporary descriptions.

THE SIDE PLATE OF THE HERCULES FOUNTAIN WITH THE COAT OF ARMS OF KING MATTHIAS

THE LION FOUNTAIN, *reconstruction (Ernő Szakál)*

The specific form of the fountain follows the structure of the 14th—c. fountain on the same spot, but the details were already late Gothic. The fragments of the old one were built into the back panel of the 15th—c. fountain.

The one—step tall base of bricks and irregular red marble slabs shows hasty work. The lion figures serving as the bases of the pillars were already carefully accomplished. Each of the lions, which symbolize the evil, is forced down by two dogs (to symbolize loyalty and loyal subjects) to bear the weight of the fountain. The fountain symbolizes Matthias' empire. On the sides of the baldachin supported by the pillars the coats of arms of Matthias' countries were to be seen: those of Hungary and Dalmatia can be recognized. On the back panel the coats of arms of the aristocracy were to be seen; some have remained: those of the family of the King's mother — Szilágyi and the supporters of the Hunyadi family — Szapolyai. Matthias' personal coat of arms with the raven was carved on the covering plate of the baldachin. Around it the date of the construction can be read on a twisting ribbon. Unfortunately the corner describing the decade was destroyed, so it can only be guessed from the data of the history of the palace construction that the year was 1483. The fountain was crowned with a crenel, the baldachin and the back panel are richly ornamented with late Gothic foliage. Lions appear not only at the base but also on the hanging supports and as the two spouts.

The red marble lunette, which as the local is said 'had been once in the Visegrád chapel', was found in a mansion near Esztergom, on the left bank of the Danube, in Karva (Slovakia) in 1863. It must have been found about a century earlier during the demolition of the ruins of the palace.

THE 'VISEGRÁD MADONNA'

It may have embellished the top of one of the side altars or the tabernacle. It was made of red marble mined in Gerecse, which proves that it was carved in Hungary. Other works of its sculptor are known from Italy. The Visegrád Madonna is a typical representative of a 15th—c. type of depiction. Several similar works have remained but their artistic level differ greatly. The Visegrád copy is one of the weakest pieces, which illustrates that however generously King Matthias donated Renaissance art, he was only able to attract second— or third—rate Italian artists, and when he wanted to buy first—class works, he had to buy them in Italy.

THE MATTHIAS PERIOD STOVE WITH THE COATS OF ARMS
OF KING MATTHIAS, *reconstruction*

The stove imitates the structure of Gothic towers. Its foundation was a walled low plinth covered with yellowish brown tiles with tracery and shields. This was closed with a green glazed cornice. The lower, brick—shaped part containing the fire—plane was also built of green glazed tiles. The lower row is square, its closed front panel consisted of delicately shaped tiles with reliefs depicting lions lying under trees. Above them there were rectangular tiles with angels holding shields on the barrel—shaped back—side. The corners were decorated with small clay figures in exquisite niches. One of them depicting the Archangel Gabriel has been found. Above the clay figures the corners were cut slantwise and covered with shields. Above this was to the upper, slimmer part of the stove; its plan was a rectangle with rounded corners. It consisted of taller tiles with niches; in the lower row the angel motive was used, in the upper ones the tiles depicted three types of armed knights. All of them appeared in front of late Gothic foliage; the first type with sabres and shield called 'pavese', the second with lances and the third with spears and round shields with a distorted head. The row of green tiles was lined with yellow semi—cylindrical tiles. Above this was the green concave cornice ornamented with festoons, then the gable from pierced ogived tiles. In the green glazed frames ornamented with unglazed foliage, yellow glazed angel figures were standing with unglazed shields. Behind the gable erected the green and yellow tent roof of three kinds of tracery tiles, the double point of which was embellished with a finial each.

The coats of arms of the stove depict partly those of the countries and supporters of King Matthias, thus following the pattern of the coats of arms on the bay window and fountains; and there are some which represent counties and towns and there is even the imperial ensign with the double—eagle of the Hapsburgs, never owned by Matthias. The latters suggest the Hungarian king's claim for the Hapsburg estates and the imperial title in the rivalry with Emperor Frederick III of the Hapsburg House, as when the refurnishing of the Visegrád palace was going on, i.e. when the stove was made, too, in the second part of the 1480s, Matthias' foreign policy was focusing exactly on these problems.

THE CLOISTER OF THE FRANCISCAN FRIARY, *reconstruction*

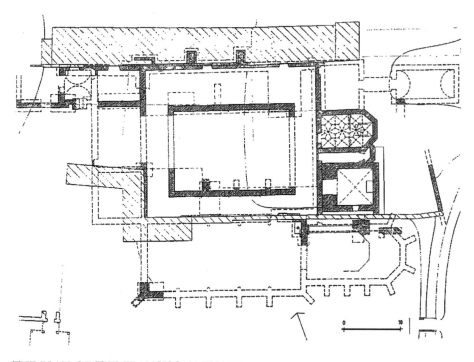

THE PLAN OF THE FRANCISCAN FRIARY

The church of the friary built beside the palace in the 1420s was vaulted originally as well. The lateral thrust of the vault was counteracted by buttresses with flyers over the cloister walk on the northern side of the nave. Stone benches ran along both inner sides of the southern cloister walk with open lancet windows. A door opened into the nave of the church from the eastern part of the cloister. The garth was east—western oriented and rectangular probably due to the lack of space. The northern cloister walk was considerably wider than the other but there was no building beside it. This part and the western section of the friary were two—levelled. The chapter house was situated in the eastern wing.

In the middle of the 15th c. the buildings of the friary became unusable, so in 1473 King Matthias requested the permission of the Pope to build a friary for the Franciscans.

The ruined Observant Franciscan friary was reconstructed by Wladislas II in the first decade of the 16th c. In 1513 the chapter of the Observant Order was held in the Visegrád friary.

During the reconstruction, the old chancel of the church was pulled down, and a new larger one was built with ribbed vaulting. The chapter house and the cloister were covered with net vaulting and cross vaulting. The buildings were ornamented with Renaissance door and window frames. The leader of the construction arrived most probably from Bohemia.

In 1535 the friary was inhabited by eight friars including the guardian, four of whom were priests.

The active friary was last mentioned in October 1540.

TOURNAMENTS

No social event can characterize the Middle Ages better than tournaments. From the 12th century they were widespread and became longer and longer, more and more complicated and splendid; they were the scene of several events: military practice, parades, entertainment the audience, meeting point for friends and enemies, lovers and young knight searching for glory. As time passed the military function was overshadowed by the magnificance of ceremonies: waving flags, shields and helmets with coats of arms, embroided saddle—cloth and blankets, inlaid armours, bugle—calls, praising and inciting platitudes of heralds, lords and their ladies wearing their most beautiful clothes and sitting on tall carpeted stands. That was what tournaments meant in their golden age, at the end of the 14th and at the beginning of the 15th centuries.

The culture which created tournaments was familiar in Hungary as well, even though it arrived here later. During the reign of our kings of west European houses it had its great age here as well.

There are quite early reports about the knighting of our kings: about the ceremony the origin of which may be rooted in customs of German tribes, which meant for a young nobleman that he became an adult and was allowed to join the warriors. We know that King St Stephen was invested with a sword by one of his Bavarian knights before the battle with Koppány, and chronicles speak about the knighting of Géza II in 1146

and Ladislas IV (Cuman) in 1278, they both gained their swords before their first battle as well.

The retinues and courts of queens played a very significant role in the formation of court culture in Hungary; somehow they seem to have been more important in the cultural life of the country than it could be supposed. German, Italian and French knights often arrived in Hungary with the escorts of the queens as well as with the crusadors crossing the country (e.g. Conrad III and Luis VII with the second crusade or the ill—fated leader of the third crusade, Emperor Frederick Barbarossa). King Béla III was especially excellent from this point of view, both of his wives were in close contact with outstanding personalities of court life (cf. the chapter about him). In the court of his son, King Emeric, two celebrated troubadours, Peire Vidal and Geulcelm Faidit lived as beloved and highly appreciated guests for several years.

The institution of court knighthood only became general in the time of our Angevin kings: Charles Robert's knights and magisters belonged to his household and had important offices: they were generals, barons, castellans or bailiffs. In their homes they also tried to imitate the royal court: palaces — with at least one heated room and often with glazed windows — were built beside the 13th—century donjons. They were good patrons, too: they ordered codices (e.g. Demeter Nekcsei, treasurer, the Bible in Bologne) or built, enlarged and redecorated churches.

Tournaments were first organized in the time of Emeric and Andrew II, but they only became regular in Charles

Robert's household of Italian and French character. The arrangement of tournaments were given an impetus during the reign of Charles Robert's son, Luis the Great, the 'knight king' especially by his campaigns in Naples, where the Hungarians spent years with fights, and also take part in tournaments. Some of them did not return home even after the fights were over: Miklós Toldi was the deputy of the English leader of the infamous Alba Societas, White band, mercenaries including severals other Hungarians.

King Sigismund, later Sovereign of the Holy Roman Empire followed his father—in—law's example: he often participated in the tournaments himself as well. A report about one of the tournaments in Buda says that the King fought with nine opponents without a break in one day. His tournament suit has remained in the book heraldry of the Order of the Golden Fleece as Hungarian royal clothes.

An experienced French knight, Bertrandon de la Brocquerie also visited Sigismund's court. He kept a diary about his journeys, in which he also wrote about the wedding of Miklós Garai, the son of the palatine. A tournament was also arranged on this occasion, in which the groom took part as well. As it turns out from Brocquerie's description tournaments in Hungary were slightly different from those in the western countries; the reasons for this may have originated in ancient Hungarian customs. 'The knights riding small horses in low saddles are clad in suits of armour, chain armour or breast—plates and used very short lances. ... It often happens that both combat-

ants fall off their horses. Here it really turns out who has a steady seat on the horse. ... The horses and saddles are drawn before the tournament ...' All this differs from the general style of tournaments which were certainly also exercised in Hungary, as foreign knights also came here and they were used to the 'classic' syle; so the above—mentioned were probably only typical of social events similar to Garai's wedding.

The classical tournaments lasted three days but were often longer because of the repeated events: the tournament on the occasion of the wedding of Wladislas II and Ann Candele, French princess lasted twelve days in Buda.

On the first day of the tournament a parade of helmets was held in a large, open, arcaded courtyard, most often in the cloister of a monastery; the ceremonial court of the Visegrád palace was also suitable for the purpose. The helmets and coats of arms of the participants were exhibited, which provided an opportunity for both the opponents and the audience to learn who would be participating. This was also the last time for the judges to suspend someone, though this only rarely happened.

The tournament held on a c. 60 m x 50 m ground separated from the audience with double fencing began at ten o'clock of the actual first day. The participants gathered in two groups behind two tauntened ropes; and after the rules were introduced, the Knight of Honour chosen by the ladies the previous night cut the ropes and the struggle began: first they fought with lances then with swords. It was in the rules that if someone fell off the horse, he was only allowed to fight with a similarly unmounted opponent; anyone breaking this rule was disqualified as well as those who injured a horse. The shield—bearers of the knights were allowed to help their lords in trouble, but they only wore light leather armour lest they joined the combatants.

The struggle generally lasted till nightfall; at the evening banquet the best fighters of the two teams were presented with prizes and it was also announced who — 6—12 knights — could participate in the next day's joust.

A railing separated the sides of the two opponents; in the 15th century it was rather broad—cloth on a wooden frame as there were several accidents when the knights in their heavier and heavier armour knocked against the wooden railing. The lance used only in tournaments was about 3.5 m long, it had to be held with the right hand and pointed at the shield in the opponent's left hand. It had a crown—shaped tip that it should not cause fatal injuries (lances used in battles were spiky). The aim of the participant was not to push the opponent out of his saddle — Brocquerie mentioned this as a different style — but to break his own lance on the opponent's shield and while avoiding his tilt. If the opponent fell of his horse, extra points were given. The judges gave high points, too, when the two lances met 'crown with crown' or there was a touch on the opponent's helmet. The knight breaking the most lances was also awarded a prize. The winner of this day was announced at the evening banquet.

◄≪THE RED MARBLE TOMB OF STI-BOR STIBORICI, *the 1530s*. The armour of one of King Sigismund's lords shows the contemporary wear: brassard, cubitiére, cuisse and jambeau, breastplate with chains for the weapons — if the weapon was knocked out of the knight's hand, he did not lose it. The helmet is on his left and the shield with his coat of arms on his right.

KNIGHT WITH A LANCE *Green glazed tile from the secong half of the 15th century*
≫→

HERALD WITH A FLAG AND AN ARMORIAL SHIELD *Green glazed stove tile*. Sigismund period. Heralds officiated at tournaments: announced the start and finish, recorded the participants, supervised the fairness of the struggle and last but not least urged the audience to give donations. ≫→

KNIGHT WITH A LANCE Green glazed tiles from the 'knight—figured' stove. The stove embellished the palace of Ladislas V or King Matthias, which proves that tournaments had their golden age in the 15th—c. Hungary.

STOVE TILE WITH KING SIGISMUND The beginning of the 15th c. Sigismund, who ascended the Hungarian throne through his marriage, was brought up in the court of Luis the Great, where he learned the ideals of the 'knight king'. During his journeys he visited several royal and princely courts. In Buda and Visegrád he tried to introduce the customs he saw in France, Burgundy and England.

CARVED BONE SADDLES The scenes depict ladies and knights clad in Burgundy court wear dancing, singing and playing music. All this belonged to banquets after tournaments.

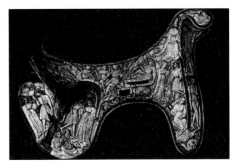

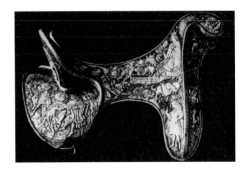

CHRONOLOGY

1000—1038 The reign of King Stephen I (Saint)

1002 Visegrád mentioned first in the foundation document of the Veszpém bishopric 1046—1060 The reign of Andrew I The foundation of the Basilite monastery of St Andrew

1063—1074 The reign of King Solomon

1074—1077 The reign of King Géza I

1077—1095 The reign of King Ladislas I (Saint)

1221 Benedicines take over the Visegrád St Andrew's monastery

1241—1242 Mongol invasion

c. 1247 The building of the Visegrád upper castle begins

1251 Queen Mary dates a charter in Visegrád; the building of the upper castle is finished

1285 The Visegrád settlers, 'Hospes' are first mentined

1301—1305 The reign of King Wenceslas

1301 King Wenceslas' troops then Máté Csák occupy Visegrád

1301—1342 The reign of Charles Robert

1317 The supporters of Charles Robert capture the Visegrád castle from Máté Csák

1321 Máté Csák dies

1323 Charles Robert moves the royal seat from Temesvár to Visegrád

1325 The church in the castle is consecrated to St John the Baptist; the rebuilding of the castle is finished

1330 Felician Zach' assassination attempt against the royal family in Charles Robert's town house

1333 The monastery of St Andrew is rebuilt

1335 Kings meet in Visegrád: Charles Robert — Hungarian king, John — Czech king, Casimir III — Polish king and the Teuton Order, Charles — Moravian marquis, Rudolf I — Saxon prince and Boleslo III — Prince of Silesia and Legnica

1342 Charles Robert dies in the Visegrád upper castle

1342—1382 The reign of Luis I (the Great)

1349 The royal court moves to Buda

1355 The royal court moves back to Visegrád

1356 The Visegrád royal chamber is first mentioned

1366 Pope Urban V gives permit of indulgence to St Mary's Church built in the Visegrád palace of King Luis and Queen Mother Elizabeth

after 1372 The rebuilding of the Visegrád palace begins

1373 King Luis dates a charter in the Visegrád royal palace

1382—1395 The reign of Queen Mary

1385—1386 The reign of Charles II (the Small)

1386 Charles II injured seriously in Buda is taken to Visegrád, where he dies

1387—1437 The reign of Sigismund of Luxemburg

1391 Charles II excommunicated earlier is properly buried in the Visegrád monastery of St Andrew

c. 1400 The building of the new Visegrád palace is finished

after 1405 The royal court moves to Buda

after 1424 The new Observant Franciscan friary founded earlier by Sigismund in the place of the palace chapel is built near the new palace

1437—1439 The reign of Albert (Hapsburg)

1439 Albert falls ill with dysentery, is treated in the Visegrád palace, leaves Visegrád and dies in Neszmély

1440—1444 The reign of Wladislas (Jagello)

1440 Mrs Helena Kottanner, the lady—in—waiting of Queen Elizabeth steals the crown for the infant Ladislas V from the Visegrád upper castle False money is coined in the mint of the palace

1440—1457 The reign of Ladislas V (Hapsburg) The King stays in Hungary only in the last two years of his reign

1458—1490 The reign of Matthias I (Hunyadi)

1461—1464 The Visegrád estate is in the hand of Catherine Podebrad

1476 The Visegrád royal estate is under the authority of the Buda court marshal, the rebuilding of the upper castle and the palace begins The wedding of King Matthias and Beatrix

1479 A cellar is built in the garden of the palace

before 1481 The bay window with coats of arms, decorating the facade of the palace is finished

1483 The Lion fountain is built

1484 The cloister of the reception court is vaulted

after 1485 The palace is furnished

1490—1516 The reign of Wladislas II (Jagello)

1492 Parliament decides the Visegrád upper castle is given to the guards of the crown

1493 The monastery of St Andrew is taken over and rebuilt by the Paulines with the help of Tamás Bakócz

before 1513 The King rebuilds the Observant Franciscan friary beside the palace

1516—1526 The reign of Luis II (Jagello)

1523 Luis issues a charter in the Visegrád palace

1526 After the Mohács battle the treasures of the Visegrád palace are put in security in Pozsony (Bratislava) from the Turks; the upper castle is defended by the inhabitants fleeing there and the Márianosztra Paulines against a Turkish raiding troop

1526—1540 The reign of John of Szapolya

1526—1564 The reign of Ferdinand I (Hapsburg)

1527 The army of Ferdinand I occupies Visegrád

1532 The army of John of Szapolya occupies Visegrád

1539 King John spends the summer with his wife Isabel in the renewed Visegrád palace

1540 Ferdinand I's army occupies the upper castle 1541 The Turks occupy Buda

1544 The Turks occupy Visegrád

1595 The Christian troops lay a succesful siege to the Visegrád castle

1605 The castle surrenders to the Turks

1684 The troops of Charles of Lorraine occupy the castle

1685 After a hard battle the Visegrád castle is in Turkish hand again

1686 The Turks leave and destroy the castle

c. 1740—1750 The ruins of the palace are pulled down by the Stahremberg family

1762 The farm buildings of the Visegrád crown estate are built on one part of the area of the palace

1871—1878 József Viktorin, the Visegrád parson, initiates and Imre Henszlmann leads the excavations in the castle; the recon-

SELECTED BIBLIOGRAPHY

GENERAL

Dercsényi, Dezső: Visegrád műemlékei (Architectural Monuments of Visegrád). Budapest 1951
Héjj, Miklós: Visegrád, Budapest 1957
Dercsényi, Dezső—Héjj, Miklós. Visegrád in: Pest megye műemlékei II., Budapest 1958. pp 396—480
Balogh, Jolán: A művészet Mátyás király korában (Art during King Matthias's reign) I—II., Budapest1966. I. pp 205—251., II., pp 151—218, 244—273.
Huszár, Lajos: A visegrádi pénzverde a középkorban (The Visegrád mint in the Middle Ages) Folia Archaelogica XVII. (1966—1967) pp 195—204.
Buzás, Gergely—Szőke, Mátyás: A visegrádi vár és királyi palota a XIV—XV. században (The Visegrád castle and royal palace) in: Castrum Bene 2/1992. Budapest 1992. pp 132—156.
Medieval Visegrád, Royal castle, palace, town and Franciscan friary, Edited by József Laszlovszky, Disserationes Pannonicae ex Instituto Archaelogico Universitatis de Rolando Eötvös Nominate Budapestiensis Provenientes Series III. Volume 4. Edited by József Laszlovszky Budapest 1995.

ROMAN AGE

Soproni, Sándor: A visegrádi római tábor és középkori vár, (The Visegrád Roman camp and medieval castle) Archaelógiai Értesítő 81. 1954.
Gróf, Péter—Gróh, Dániel: Római építészeti emlékek Visegrád térségében (Roman architectural monuments in Visegrád) Műemlékvédelem 1995/2. pp 61—68.

EARLY MIDDLE AGES

Kovalovszki, Júlia: A Visegrád várkerti Árpád-kori falukutatásról, in: A magyar falu régésze, Méri István (1911—1976), Edited by Kovalovszki Júlia 1986. pp 61—63.
Szőke, Mátyás: Visegrád, ispánsági központ (Visegrád, a county centre) (Tájak Korok Múzeumok Kiskönyvtára) Budapest 1986.
Kovalovszki, Júlia: Az Árpád-kori Visegrád. Ásatások a Várkertben. (Visegrád in the Árpádian period. Excavations in the castle garden) Műemlékvédelem 1952/2. pp 69—74.

THE CASTLE, THE TOWN AND THE FRIARY

Héjj, Miklós: A visegrádi alsóvár lakótornyának építéstörténete (The architrctural history of the donjon of the lower castle in Visegrád) Műemlékvédelem 1966/1. pp 1—9.
Sedlmayr, János: A visegrádi lakótorony helyreállitása (The reconstruction of the Visegrád donjon), Magyar Műemlékvédelem V. 1967—68, Budapest 1970 pp 315—334.
Szőke, Mátyás: Harang öntőforma köpenyrészének töredékei Visegrádról (Fragments of the clay mould for a bell from Visegrád), in: Művészet I. Lajos király korában 1342—1382. Edited by Ernő Marosi, Melinda Tóth, Lívia Varga, Székesfehérvár 1982 pp 317—324.
Schőnerné Pusztai, Ilona: Beszámoló a visegrádi fellegvárban készülő rekonstrukciós munkáról (Report about the reconstruction in the Visegrád upper castle), Műemlékvédelem 1983/4 pp 225—241.
Szőke, Mátyás—Buzás, Gergely: A visegrádi Alsóvár a XIII. században (The Visegrád lower castle in the 13th c.), in: Castrum Bene 1989, Gyöngyös 1990 pp 121—134.
Buzás, Gergely—Szőke, Mátyás: Visegrád, Fellegvár (Visegrád, Upper castle) Tájak Korok Múzeumok Kiskönyvtára 250. 6. revised edition 1994.

Buzás, Gergely: Visegrád, Alsóvár (Visegrád, Lower castle) (Tájak Korok Múzeumok Kiskönyvtára 202.), 4. revised edition 1995.

Iván, László: Régészeti kutatások a visegrádi fellegvárban 1984—1994 (Archaelogical research in the Visegrád upper castle 1984—1994), Műemlékvédelem 1995/2. 75—80.

Bozóki, Lajos: Adalékok a visegrádi alsóvár építés- és helyreállítás–történetéhez (Some data of the history of the building and reconstruction of the Visegrád lower castle) Műemlékvédelem 1995/2. pp 81—97.

Szőke, Mátyás: Adatok a középkori Visegrád történetéhez és helyrajzához (Some data to the history and topography of the medieval Visegrád) in: Középkori régészetünk újabb eredményei és időszerű feladatai. Edited by István Fodor, László Selmeczi, Szeged 1985, pp 285—309.

Buzás, Gergely—Laszlovszky, József—Papp, Szilárd—Szekér, György—Szőke, Mátyás: A visegrádi ferences kolostor (The Visegrád Franciscan friary) in: Koldulórendi építészet a középkori Magyarországon, Studies (Művészettörténet-Műemlékvédelem) Budapest 1994, Edited by Andrea Haris, pp 281—304.

THE ROYAL PALACE

Schulek, János: Mátyás király visegrádi palotájának diszudvara (The ceremonial court of the Visegrád palace of King Matthias), Szépművészet II. 1941 pp 304—306.

Schulek, János: Visegrád, Mátyás király palotája (Visegrád, the palace of King Matthias), Budapest 1941.

Zsitvay, Tibor: A visegrádi királyi palota és díszudvar feltárása (The excavatiom of the Visegrád royal palace and the ceremonial court) Budapest 1942.

Meller, Péter: La fontana di Mattia Corvino a Visegrád Instituto Ungherese di Storia dell'Arte Firenze Annuario 1947. pp 47—73, 30—40, 42.

Balogh, Jolán: Die Ausgrabungen in Visegrád, Österreichische Zeitschrift für Dekmalpflege IV. 1950 pp 41—50.

Héjj, Miklós: Beszámoló a visegrádi Mátyás palota 1952. évi feltárási munkáiról (The Visegrád palace of King Matthias. Riport about the excavations), Archaelógiai Értesítő 1953 pp 64—67.

Holl, Imre: A visegrádi palota kápolnájának padozata (The pavement of the chapel in the palace of Visegrád) Archaelógiai Értesítő 1954 pp 192—196.

Szakál, Ernő: Mátyás király oroszlános kútjának rekonstrukciója (The reconstruction of the Lion fountain of King Matthias) Művészettörténeti Értesítő VIII. 1959 pp 239—250.

Szakál, Ernő: A visegrádi Anjou-kori királyi palota gótikus kútházának rekonstrukciója (The reconstruction of the Gothic fountain in the Angevin period royal palace in Visegrád) Magyar Műemlékvédelem IV. Budapest 1969 pp 159—186.

Héjj, Miklós: A visegrádi királyi palota (The Visegrád royal palace) Budapest 1970.

Szakál, Ernő: A visegrádi királyi palota Anjou-kori falikútjának rekonstrukciója (The reconstruction of the Angevin period fountain in the Visegrád royal palace), Magyar Műemlékvédelem VI. Budapest 1972 pp 345—372.

Héjj, Miklós: Ausgrabungsbericht über die Erschliessung des könilglichen Wohnpalastes zu Visegrád: Nord- und Donauflügelsektor. Folia Archaeologica 26, 1975 pp 191—197.

Héjj, Miklós: Visegrád, Királyi palota (Visegrád, The royal palace) (Tájak Korok Múzeumok Kiskönyvtára 11.) 1979

Buzás, Gergely: A visegrádi királyi palota (The Visegrád royal palace) Valóság 1990/91. pp 91—101

Buzás, Gergely: Visegrád, királyi palota 1. A kápolna és az északkeleti palota (Visegrád, royal palace 1. The chapel and the north—eastern palace) (Lapidarium Hungaricum 2.), Budapest 1990.

Buzás, Gergely: A visegrádi királyi palota Mátyás-kori építészeti kőfaragványai. Katalógus (A catalogue of the Matthias period architectural stone carvings from the palace of Visegrád) Altum Castrum 1. Visegrád 1991

Réti, Mária: Visegrád és a magyarországi reneszánsz (Visegrád and the Renaissance in Hungary), Dunakanyar 1992 pp 8—12

Buzás, Gergely: A visegrádi királyi palota ásatása (The excavation of the Visegrád royal palace), Archaeológiai Értesítő 1991 pp 63—84

Buzás, Gergely: A visegrádi királyi palota déli épülettömbjének feltárása (The excavation of the southern building of the Visegrád royal palace), Műemlékvédelmi Szemle 1992/2 pp 32—43, pictures 11—15

Buzás, Gergely—Lővei, Pál: A visegrádi királyi palota Mátyás-címeres kályhája (The stove with the coat of arms of Matthias in the Visegrád royal palace), in: Horler Miklós hetvenedik születésnapjára, tanulmányok, Művészettörténet—Műemlékvédelem IV. OMVH Budapest 1993 pp 191—217

Réti, Mária: Visegrád reneszánsz szobrászatának újabb kutatásai (The latest research of the Renaissance sculpture of Visegrád) in: Horler Miklós hetvenedik születésnapjára, tanulmányok, Művészettörténet—Műemlékvédelem IV. OMVH Budapest 1993 Edited by Pál Lővei

Balla, Árpád: Palota a föld alatt. A visegrádi királyi palota ásatása 1934—1944 (Palace under the earth. The excavations of the Visegrád royal palace) Altum Castrum 3. Visegrád 1993

Buzás, Gergely: Visegrád, Királyi palota (Visegrád, the royal palace) Tájak Korok Múzeumok Kiskönyvtára 11., 8th revised edition 1993

Buzás, Gergely: The Royal Palace at Visegrád, The Hungarian Quarterly 35. Summer 1994 pp 98—109

A visegrádi királyi palota kápolnája és északkeleti épülete (The chapel and the north—eastern building of the Visegrád royal palace) Visegrád Régészeti Monográfiái 1. Edited by Gergely Buzás, Visegrád 1994

Buzás, Gergely—Lővei, Pál: A visegrádi királyi palota címeres zárterkélye (The bay window with coats of arms in the Visegrád royal palace), Műemlékvédelem 1995/2 pp 98—112

MUSEUMS AND SIGHTS

The ruins of the late Roman fortress on Sibrik Hill and the Árpádian perod bailiff castle
Open all the year

Árpádian period archdiocese church
Not open to the public

Lower castle — Salamon–torony (Solomon's tower)
(Exhibitions of the MKM Mátyás Király Múzeum)
Open: May to September 9 am to 4.30 pm, closed on Mondays
Exhibitions: The 14th–c. fountain of the royal palace.
King Matthias' stone carving workshop
The history of Visegrád

Royal palace
(Exhibitions of the MKM Mátyás Király Múzeum) Fő u. 23—27.
Open: 9 am to 4.30 pm, closed on Mondays;
Exhibitions and sights: The ruins of the Royal Palace
Museum of stonework finds
Collection of tombs

Franciscan friary
Fő u. 39—43.
Not open to the public

Upper castle
Open: spring to autumn 9 am to 6 pm.
Exhibitions: The history of the castle
Man and nature (Hunting. Old ways of life)

BUDA

EARLIER HISTORY

In the Middle Ages Buda was the youngest among the royal residential towns of Hungary. Some remains from the period before the devastation of the Mongol invasion refer to the fact that the present Várhegy (Castle Hill) was already sparsely populated, but there certainly was no proper settlement here, though the location was suilable. Here the southern ranges of the Buda Hills last reach the Danube, and Várhegy with its flat and wide plateau but steep sides and the tall and rocky Gellérthegy protrude from the plain and the neighbouring valleys. The roads had led to the other side of the Danube, to the Pest plain and further since ancient times, as it was the easiest to cross the river here in the short reach between the long Szentendre Island and Csepel Island. Important ferries developed in the valley entrances at both ends of Várhegy, south of the ferries of Aquincum and the later Óbuda: in the north the Jenő ferry (named after the village, Jenő on the other side of the river) a bit downwards from the present Margaret Bridge, and in the south the Pest ferry at the end of the valley of the medieval brook St. Paul (today Ördögárok) a bit upwards from the present Elizabeth Bridge. The rare natural resource, the thermal springs at the foot of the hills increased the significance of both ferries as they ensured permanent winter harbours as well.

The remains of the earliest settlement from the Copper Age can be found in Víziváros; and there was a settlement on Várhegy in the early Bronze Age. Later the Celtic eraviscus tribe chose the steep Gellérthegy to build the centre of their tribe here, which was the first fortified settlement.

The Roman conquerers advancing as far as the Danube in the 1st century AD immediately recognized the importance of the place: they took control of the Celtic oppidum, and rose military camps for their troops to protect the border and the ferries. Already during the time of the conquest or a little later a camp of a auxiliary troop was built at the northern foot of Várhegy, on the flat area of the present Víziváros, to control the ferry here and to watch the Celtic settlement at the southern ferry. The wooden walls of the camp were soon replaced with stone buildings which were used till the 4th century.

During the time of migrations the area lost its population, even the ruins of the Roman buildings did not attract the peoples coming one after the other to settle here; the situation did not change after the Hungarian conquest either. Only the bare and rocky hill witnessed the martyrdom of St. Gellért, when the bishop of Csanád, who wanted to cross the river, was captured by pagan rioters. The vicinity of the ferries kept their important role, but the early royal centres and the cores of the future towns developed in the area of Óbuda and — on the other side — Pest. On the Buda side there were only smaller settlements in the attraction of these centres: first of all

Kisebb Pest (Smaller Pest) opposite to Pest, in the language of its German settlers Kreinfeld (later Alhéviz) at the feet of Gellérthegy and Várhegy, and Gézavására (later Felhéviz) at the ferry near the Roman ruins, at the north side of Várhegy.

THE FOUNDATION OF THE TOWN

In April 1241 the Mongol troops occupied and burned the town of Pest (its German name was Ofen), which was a flourishing German 'hospes' settlement. In winter the same happened to the castle, chapter and the town of Buda (i.e. Óbuda as called later), the early ecclesiastical centre settled among the Roman ruins. In spring of the following year after the sudden death of the great Khan the Mongols left the country, but their return was to be excpected any time. This urged King Béla IV, who escaped from the Mongols, to build a castle on the hill (now called Várhegy) so far only sparsely populated, opposite Pest, and move the German settlers of Pest, with their privilages, here.

During the Middle Ages the official name of the settlement was Castrum Novi Montis Pestiensis, i.e the castle of Pest Újhegy (new hill), which — from a castle built to give protection againts the Mongols — became a quickly—developing economic centre, a free royal town, a permanent royal residence. The fast development of the new centre is also marked by the fact that it even acquired the name of its predecessor: the name of the settlement built on the hill was Buda, in German Ofen, from now on.

The character of the town was de-termined by the Mongol threat, for centuries. The first step was to build the ramparts of the town around the hill, with towers at regular intervals; then in the enclosed plateau the streets were marked, the sites measured, and parish churches (the Church of Our Lady for the Germans and the Church of Mary Magdalen for the Hungarians), friaries (Franciscan and Dominican) and the civic buildings (the Town Hall, the Kammerhof i.e. royal mansion) built. The bank of the Danube was also populated from Felhéviz to Alhéviz (i.e. from today's Margaret Bridge to Tabán), as commerce was pursued through the ferries here.

During the foundation most of the citizens of the town were German, the leading strata of the society came from them: both the judge (who, at the biginning, was the rector as well as the castellan) and the council of twelve members were all rich Germans who were first of all long—distance drapers. The number and the economic importance of the Hungarians lagged far behind.

THE ROYAL COURT AND BUDA IN THE ÁRPÁDIAN AND ANGEVIN AGE

After the foundation, the more and more developing town and its fortress soon housed the royal court as well. From the end of the 13th century several gatherings of national importance were held here; and Andrew III, the last king of the House of Árpád, chose the Franciscan friary as his burial place. The royal residence was the building complex called Kammerhof in German, which has not been excavated yet. Its name suggests that similarly to Visegrád and other places abroad the royal mint was here as well. The Kammerhof or 'old royal house' rose in the north—eastern corner of the town, and it had a separate gatehouse.

After the death of the last king of the House of Árpád, in the fights for the succession to the throne the town was against Charles Robert of Naples; and supported the son of the Czech king, Wenceslas, then the Bavarian Otto. The resistance was so big that in 1304 the priests of the town excommunicated not only Charles Robert to be king later but Benedict XI as well, who supported him. That means the town was on the wrong side. Though its economic importance constantly grew in the following hundred years, the royal court moved to Visegrád, which was only known about its strong castle till then. The court stayed in Buda only for a short time, between 1347 and 1355, during King Luis the Great's campaigns to Naples and Lithuania, most possibly in the old royal mansion as the King built a royal chapel in honour of St. Martin here in the second half of the 1340s.

BUDA, THE ROYAL SEAT AND THE CAPITAL OF HUNGARY

At the end of the 14th century the advantages of the rich town attracted the royal court so it moved back to Buda, together with its offices, which caused considerable changes in the life of the town at the beginning of the 15th century. From the end of the 1370s King Luis the Great started enormous palace constructions which were still enlarged by his successor, Sigismund I (of Luxemburg). In 1381 King Luis gave the Kammerhof away; and in 1408 King Sigismund moved his court and government offices to Buda. From this time on, the country was ruled from the new royal castle till the Turkish invasion. Thus besides its economic power the town received all the advantages of being the social and political centre. More and more ecclesiastical and civil dignitaries bought houses here to be able to arrange their cases at the court; more and more merchants settled here, they were able to satisfy the luxury needs and demands of the court (there was a street, for example, which was named after Italian merchants). The buildings were enlarged and improved, new churches and chapels were founded (e.g. the provostry of St. Sigismund, Garai Chapel), the existing ones were enlarged and modernized and the suburbs were expanding. With the economic boom and the court moving here, the Hungarian middle class started to grow and strengthen. The rivalry between the two nationatities led to constant litigation, finally, in 1439, to disturbances. The tension was tried to be lessened with a reform according to which the Hungarian and German burghers elected six—six members into the council; and the judge was Hungarian respectively German in succession, chosen every year. The fact that the royal court was in Buda resulted that the history of the town intertwined with the history of the kingdom; and from now on several events of national importance took place in Buda.

The Royal Seat Becomes a Turkish Castle

The failure came round together with the collapse of the kingdom.

On 29 August 1526 Sultan Suleiman II inflicted a crushing defeat upon the Hungarian army near Mohács. The capital, Buda, remained defenceless as from the River Drava there was no considerable fortress in the way of the invaders. The inhabitants and the royal court ran panic—stricken as they did not trust the ramparts. After this battle the aim of those who wanted to rule the kingdom was to acquire Buda; thus the role of the town was completely reconsidered, its military significance became the most important above all. The principle during the following 15 years of war was: he who owns Buda, owns the kingdom. Finally in 1541 the town was occupied by the Ottomans. So the first period of the history of Buda was over; first the German, then the Hungarian inhabitants left the town, giving room to Turkish and Southern Slav soldiers and their families: the former capital of the kingdom became the border fortress of the Turkish empire.

Buda at the Beginning of the 16th Century

1.The royal palace; 2. The royal gardens; 3. The royal stables; 4. The bronze statue of Heracles; 5. The 'Friss' Palace; 6. St. Sigismund's Church; 7. Franciscan friary; 8. Franciscan begina convent; 9. The Gate of St. John; 10. The Jewish Gate; 11. St. George's Church; 12. The market; 13. Apothecary Row; 14. The Town Hall; 15. Fountain; 16. The parish Church of Our Lady (German); 17. St. Michael's Chapel; 18. St. Ladislas' Chapel (?); 19. The cemetery; 20. Small door; 21. Dominican friary; 22. Old royal mansion — Kammerhof and St. Martin's Chapel; 23. The Synagogue; 24. The Szombat Gate; 25. The parish Church of Mary Magdalen (Hungarian); 26. The Chapel of All—Saints (?); 27. Austin friary; 28. Salt—depot; 29. The parish Church of St. Peter Martyr; 30. Corpus Christi Chapel (?); 31. The convent of the Order of Carmelites (?); 32. Taschental; 33. Tótfalu; 34. Logod; 35. Alhéviz; 36. Felhéviz; 37. St. Lazarus' Chapel (?); 38. The scaffold; 39. The market in Felhéviz; 40. The Pest ferry

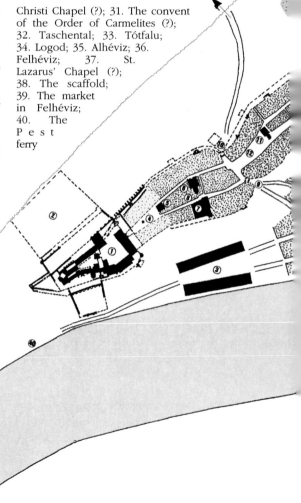

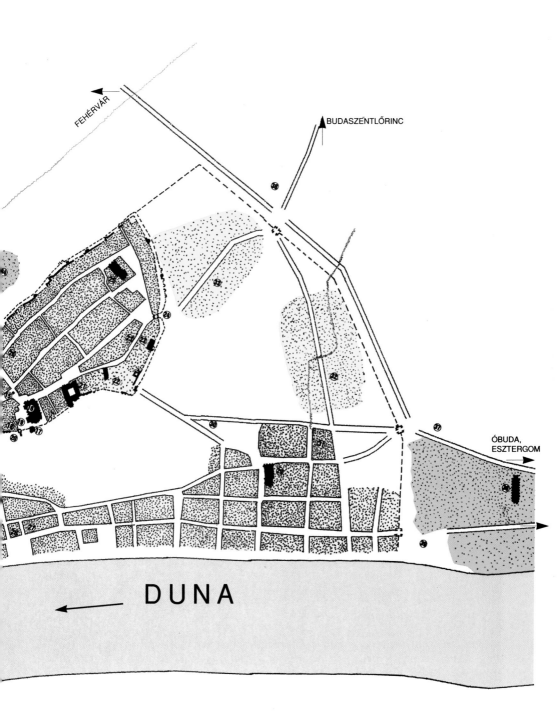

FEHÉRVÁR

BUDASZENTLŐRINC

ÓBUDA,
ESZTERGOM

DUNA

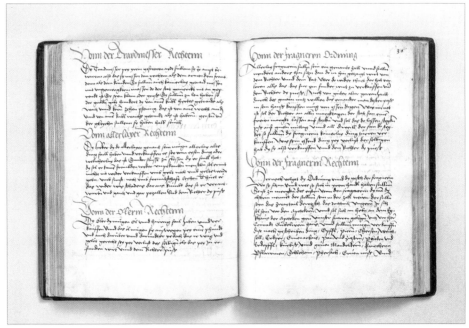

THE BUDA LAW—BOOK, i.e. 'OFNER STADTRECHT', *the book of rules and regulations in Buda, written in German, opened at the chapters dealing with the regulations on the market.*

The town law—book from the beginning of the 15th century was completely written in German, as that time the leadership of the town consisted exclusively of Germans. The original copy was destroyed during the Turkish wars when the whole Record Office of the town was devastated. Its copies, however, remained in Pozsony and Kassa, which shows that the collection of the Buda rules and regulation set a good example. In the picture the Kassa copy kept in the University Library can be seen.

THE COASTS OF ARMS OF THE TOWN OF BUDA FROM THE SZOMBAT GATE, *stone carving from the beginning of the 16th century.*

Buda inherited its coat of arms, used also in the seals of the town, together with its privileges from Pest. The ramparts, towers and the gate symbolized the independent power, protectedness and at the same time openness of the town. This general symbol can be found in the coats of arms of several Hungarian and foreign towns. The carvings with its coats of arms once reminded the new—comer that he was entering an independent town. The medieval gates among them the former Szombat Gate, now called Bécsi (Vienna) Gate were pulled down at the end of the last century.

13TH—CENTURY TOWER ON THE INNER RAMPART IN THE COURTYARD OF
THE WAR HISTORY MUSEUM

The ramparts of the fortified town — considered as castle at the beginning — surrounded
the whole plateau of the hill already at the time of its foundation, running where possible along the rocky edge of the steep hillside. Today some parts of this first wall are
well—known. On the western side long sections were excavated under the present Tóth
Árpád sétány. It was clearly visible that the wall was protected with semicircular and
square towers built in regular intervals; eight of them were dug up as far as the present
Fehérvári Gate. To the south one and in the foreground of the royal palace two other
towers have been found. On the north side, in the courtyard of the War History
Museum a semicircular and in the vicinity of the Erdélyi Bastion a part of another semicircular tower were uncovered. On the eastern side no such tower, only some parts of
the castle wall were excavated, but charters speak about towers in the wall on this side
as well. On the eastern side, which was more protected because of the river, three ecclesiastical buildings were constructed in the walls: the Dominican and Franciscan friaries
and probably the parish Church of Our Lady as well.
The shape of the plateau was a long—stretching triangle so the corners needed special
fortification. At the north—western corner some parts of a huge square tower were uncovered; but they were the remains of a later rebuilding in the Middle Ages, the original
corner of the ramparts is not known. The Kammerhof or as sources later mention the old
royal mansion was situated in the north—eastern corner. The excavations of limited size
opened up the remains of a gatehouse and a section of the ramparts from the time of the

foundation of the town. Unfortunately at the southern corner — though there was a big excavation here — the enclosure of the fortification cannot be seen, as because of the enormous buildings of the royal palace the former walls disappeared. In the 1340s, however, the town castle of Prince Stephen of the House of Anjou was built here, on the narrow protrusion of the rocky plateau. About half a century later this castle was reconstructed into a huge royal palace. Both the Kammerhof and Stephen's castle were to be found at the edge of the plateau so the town as well, which shows that it was important to be separated within the town. The Kammerhof had a gate opening to the outside of the ramparts. Both residences were built on the Danube side, and rose above the ferries and important parts of the town outside the walls; so they controlled important roads — the Danube and the traffic of the ferries. The places of the gates seem to have been planned carefully. On the narrowing part of the hill two gates opened facing each other to the market place of the Germans, to Szent György tér. In the east, looking onto the Danube was the Gate of St. John, in the west towards the vineyards and the road leading to Fehérvár was the Jewish Gate. The third gate, the 'Szombat' Gate was in the north wall opening from the market place of the Hungarians, called Szombathely, this led to the Esztergom road. The Kelenföldi Gate is only known from written sources, it must have opened onto the south; but it has not been located yet. At the end of the last century all the gates were pulled down, there have been no excavations to research them. From the remaining pictures and maps it can be stated that the gates opened from square towers and were situated a bit inwards from the imaginary straight line of the ramparts which returned to the gatehouses.

So it can be seen that the fortress built in the time of the foundation enclosed a very large area; and it was carefully planned together with the town. The protective system, which consisted of   ramparts and towers protruding outside the wall, can be considered highly developed in its time. The fortification in Buda was among the most significant constructions of King Béla IV, just like the double castle in Visegrád and the ramparts of Fehérvár.

The ramparts described above were soon surrounded with another outer wall. The time of the construction is not known; it is generally mentioned as the 'Angevin wall'. It is also possible that building a second wall was in the original plans, and it was built either together with the inner wall or a little bit later. Building double ramparts is typical of the fortification of most medieval towns: the tall inner wall fortified with towers was generally surrounded with a much lower outer wall without towers, thus they formed a passage. In this respect the ramparts of Buda served as an example.

THE SEAL OF THE BUDA RECTOR, JOHN, THE SON OF HENC, 1328.
After the foundation of the town the King appointed a rector as the head of the town, who at the same time was the castellan of the fortification. After the Mongol threat was over, the role of the rectors was taken over by judges who — at least in theory — were elected by the town. John, the son of Henc, came from one of the richest German noble families of the town; his coat of arms can be seen in their seal.

CHURCH OF OUR LADY BEFORE THE REBUILDING IN THE LAST CENTURY

The Church of Our Lady has preserved most of the remains of the medieval architecture. Today the church is known as Matthias Church, but this name only originates from the last century when the coat of arms of King Matthias from 1470 was found on the tower. The name is romantic, the patron saint of the church, however, is still the Virgin Mary. The church has kept its late—medieval character till the end of the 70s of the last century, in spite of being reconstructed during the Turkish and Baroque times. At the end of the last century (1874—1896) Frigyes Schulek, an architect, renewed the building in Romanitic style. Schulek carefully surveyed the church, so the medieval parts as well, and considered the 13th—century fragments the most valuable. To reach the desired effect he completed the building according to his own plans. He had several parts pulled down, from the medieval period as well as the Turkish and Baroque times; and had the original carved stones taken out and carved again. Schulek's recontruction meant so big changes in the original building that today it can be considered as last century work of art. The original medieval church is known from the surveys, photographs and the original stones to be found in the museum.

THE INSIDE OF THE CHURCH OF OUR LADY BEFORE THE REBUILDING IN THE LAST CENTURY

The church and the town were founded at the same time. The church was the parish church of the Germans in the Middle Ages. A royal charter from 1255 says the church is to be built, while another one from 1269 already speaks about the newly built church. Its significance incresead as the royal court often visited it as well. It is enough to mention that King Matthias had both of his wedding ceremonies here; and that after the victorious Balkan campaign of János of Hunyadi in 1444 the plundered flags were hung here, too. The parson of the church was generally appointed by the king, though this would have been the right of the burghers according to the law—book of the town. In spite of this, generally one of the clergymen of the royal court received the benefice, which meant a rich income and high rank. The parson was the archdeacon of the Buda district as well; and from 1497 he was granted special permission to wear the insignia of the prelates. Several clergymen — both Hungarians and Germans — worked with him, chaplains and rectors 'altaris'. In 1435 a document mentioned five of his chaplains and his choir masters. The secular caretaker of the church, who handled the property of the parish, always came from high—ranking burgher families. Distinguished German burghers led the Corpus Christi confraternity as well, which worked in Buda, too, similarly to other towns in Hungary.

THE CHURCH OF OUR LADY *in the 13th century*
The original church was three—aisled, with the structure of a basilica, with a transept; the side—chancels were closed in a straight line and the main chancel with the sides of a dodecagon. Two towers were planned on the facade, but it is not sure whether both were completed.

THE MARY DOORWAY
OF THE CHURCH OF OUR LADY *during the dig in the last century*

The Church was considerably rebuilt at the beginning of the 15th century. There is no exact data about the time of the reconstruction, only two pieces of informtion. In 1384 the tower collapsed during a Mass, according to the document no—one was hurt. From 1414 the permit of Pope John XXIII is known for indulgence, which he issued for the helpers of the construction work. The whole church was rebuilt. Inside a hall was formed, so the side walls were risen, and new tracery windows with four mullions were put in on the south side. The side—chancels were lengthened as far as the main chancel. On the south side there was a new, richly ornamented porch, called Mary Doorway; it has remained only in fragments but it is unique among the works of the Buda sculpture. After the construction was finished, new chapels were built to the sides of the church, in the north the sepulchral chapel of the family of Baron Garai and in the south that of Johann Ellenpeck, a Buda burgher. Both were accomplished by 1433.

After an interval of about a lifespan, King Matthias continued the construction work. To the southern side of the church, between the 4th and 6th pillars an annex was built, presumably for a royal oratory. It was then that the rebuilding of the collapsed south tower and the building of the north tower began. The coat of arms of King Matthias was placed on the south tower in 1470. The shape and the decoration of the tower are very similar to the northern tower of St. Elizabeth's Church in Kassa (Kosice, Kaschau), and so it may be considered to have been built in the style of the Vienna stone—curving lodge. It is very likely that the builder of the Kassa tower, Master Stephen built the tower of the Church of Our Lady, as his other work in Buda is known; and he died in Buda.

The doorway in the spandrel of which the death and assumption of Vigin Mary can be seen bears the stylistical characteristics of royal stone curvers.

MARY WITH THE CHILD JESUS *Red marble relief from the Church of Our Lady, c. 1480*

The fragment of the Madonna relief were found during the construction work by Schulek; but the inner decoration and the furnishings the church were already completely devastated earlier. Some fragments of the wall paintings were copied during the reconstruction, but no continuous surface was found. Besides the name of the main altar, the names of five more altars are mentioned in charters; but they all were destroyed as well. The ecclesiastical objects, which were taken to Pozsony in 1526, then brought back to Buda at the beginning of the 18th century, were lost; everything was auctioned at the order of Emperor Joseph II in 1785, and they have never been found.

Mary Magdalen's Church, which was the parish church of the Hungarian population of the town, suffered a lot of damage; so its remains are much more fragmentary. In 1686 the Christian army broke a hole in the ramparts near the church, and invaded the town under Turkish rule through it. In the heavy bombardment the church was seriously damaged, so only the tower was worth recontructing. The other ruined walls were pulled down; and on new foundations a new, Baroque church was built, mainly from the stones of the old church. During the siege in 1944—1945 the nave was ruined again by a bomb. After this only the tower was reconstructed in its original medieval form.

By the help of the several stone carvings found here and archaelogical research, the history of the building can be reconstructed.

THE TOWER OF MARY MAGDALEN'S CHURCH, *the beginning of the 16th century.*

MARY MAGDALEN'S CHURCH *in the 16th century*

At the time of the foundation of the town, the church was a small one—aisled building which differed from village churches neither in size nor in form. If we compare this simple church with the three—aisled Church of Our Lady, the different social status and position of the German and Hungarian burghers can clearly be seen in the early period of the history of the town. The tower and the gallery were only built in the first part of the 14th century. It was only reconstructed into a real town church when the Hungarian middle—class became stronger at the turn of the 14th—15th centuries. The new church was a church hall, the plan of which was generally used: it was three—aisled, its side chancels were closed with a straight line and its main chancel with the sides of a polygon. Its characteristic feature is that the nave was about square, and the length of the nave was about the same as that of the chancel. Its plan was exactly the same as that of the smaller Church of Virgin Mary, also called St. Sigismund, which stood in front of the royal palace, and which was built by King Sigismund around 1410. The proportioning and vaulting of the main chancel can be reconstructed from the fragments found; and so it can be stated that it was very close in structure and style to the Gothic chancel of the Dominican friary.

THE VAULTING OF THE FIRST LEVEL OF THE TOWER OF MARY MAGDALEN'S CHURCH, *the beginning of the 16th century*
The medieval tower of Mary Magdalen's Church, which was rebuilt in the last quarter of 15th century, can be seen today, too. The enormous tower was built in the axis of the

church, its lower levels were square, the upper ones octogonal with huge windows around, just like on the southern tower of the Church of Our Lady. Its most beautiful part is the lierne vaulting over the entrance, which is the only late Gothic vaulting in its original place in Buda. The nave was lengthened and thus joined to the tower; so the proportions of the church were changed. The nave had six sections; and new chapels were built to the side of the tower. Two dates refer to the completion of the construction work: 1496 on the entrance of the new choir and 1503 in the fragments of a fresco on the side of the tower near the nave.

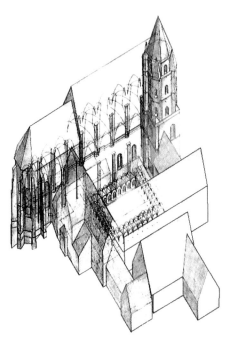

THE DOMINICAN FRIARY, *the beginning of the 16th century*
The friaries of mendicant orders played a very important role in the life of the town. At the time of the foundation of the town both the Franciscans and the Dominicans were in close contact with the royal court: King Stephen V was buried in the Dominican convent in Margaret Island, and Andrew III chose the Franciscan friary in Buda as his burial place. Later the provincialates of both orders were in Buda, where they also had colleges in the friaries. The Dominican college granted the highest qualifications in Hungary. Famous personalities of the Hungarian medieval literature lived in the Franciscan friary: Pelbárt Temesvári and Osvát Laskai.
St. Nicholas friary of the Dominicans can be found near the Church of Our Lady; with several original parts. The church was a narrow, one—aisled building with a stretched plan. The chancel to be seen in ruins today, too, originates from the turn of the 14th—15th centuries. The chancel is seperated from the nave with a rood–screen rebuilt at least twice in the Middle Ages, only its foundation level was uncovered. Today the wall of the nave on the side of the friary rises up to the vaulting. This was mostly the wall of the original 13th—century church, but the vaulting was made at the beginning of the 15th century. As it can be seen in contemporary pictures, there was a tall tower

standing beside the church. Only the two lower, square—shaped levels remained; the upper levels were octagonal. The quadrangle of the friary was accomplished at the beginning of the 14th century; later it was rebuilt and enlarged several times. The most significant of the construction work was when the cloister was vaulted, its eastern wing enlarged, so the chapter house became bigger.

From the Franciscan friary of St. John, the Evangelist, only the foundation walls have remained in the southern part of the town. The friary was already dissolved in the Turkish times; the church damaged in the sieges was pulled down after the town was reoccupied. The Baroque church of the Carmelites built in its place (today Várszinház — Castle Theatre) must have several stone carvings in its walls from the medieval church.

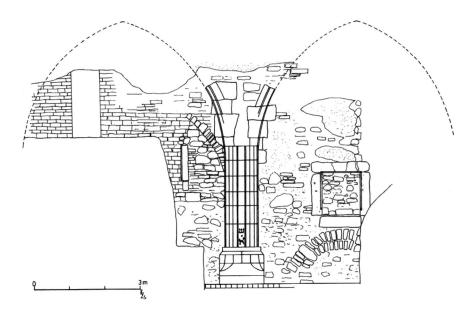

DRAWING OF THE UNCOVERED WALLS OF THE SYNAGOGUE

The Jewish community is as old as the town, the oldest gravestone from their cemetery found in Krisztinaváros, was stood in 1278. First the Jews worked in the royal mint; later they dealt with credits and commerce. It is not known where their first synagogue was; till the 1360s they lived in the southern part of the town, but then King Luis the Great ousted them from the territory of the whole kingdom. After the enormous palace was gradually built in the southern part of the town from the end of the 1370s to the 1420s, the Jews taken back were settled in the north part of the town beside the old royal mansion, the Kammerhof, given to the Order of St. Paul by King Luis in 1381. Two of their synagogues are known in this area. The older one was established in a house. Some parts of the newer one were found in the courtyard of the building at 23 Tácsics Mihály utca. It was a two—aisled building with a vaulting dividing it into four parts, similarly to the well—known medieval synagogues in Prague and Worms. The Hebrew inscripction on the middle pillar says the building was constructed in 1461. The Jewish prefect of Buda was appointed the principal of all the Jew of the country.

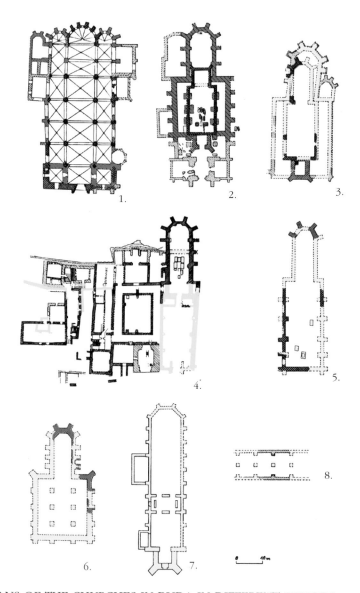

THE PLANS OF THE CHURCHES IN BUDA IN DIFFERENT PERIODS

1. The Church of Our Lady (German parish church)
2. Mary Magdalen's Church (Hungarian parish church)
3. The Church of St. Peter the Martyr (suburbian parish church)
4. St. Nicholas friary of the Dominicans
5. The Franciscan friary of St. John the Evangelist
6. St. Sigismund's Church
7. The Holy Trinity Church in Felhéviz
8. The new synagogue

☐ the first half of the 13th century (before 1241)
■ the second half of the 13th century
■ the first half of the 14th century
■ the second half of the 14th century
■ the first half of the 15th century
▨ the second half of the 15th century
☐ the first half of the 16th century

A TWO—STOREY HOUSE *(31 Úri utca)*

The rich burghers and the dignitaries having houses in the town usually lived in big, multi—storey buildings. The entrance generally opened in the axis of the facade through a wide and tall gate which was big enough for carts as well. This was necessary as most of the burghers and even several dignitaries had vineyards on the neighbouring hillsides, as this was the most valuable wine growing area of the kingdom. The wine was stored in cellars under the houses, which often had several levels. Both sides of the wide doorways were decorated with niches; the ground—floor rooms opened from here. On the ground floor workshops, stables and the rooms of the servants were to be found; the owner of the house and his family lived on the upper levels. The houses in Buda were generally multi—storey buildings; but after the sieges in the Turkish times generally just the ground—floor walls remained, only some fragments of the upper walls were found in some places.

ARCADED INNER COURTYARD *(34 Úri utca)*

HOUSE OF THE FORMER
APOTHECARY ROW *(14 Tárok utca)*
The apothecaries were small retail shops
in the market place of the town. They
were situated on the ground floor of the
houses, with huge windows through
which different goods were sold; the living quarters were on the upper floors.

NICHES

2 Országház utca, 15th century   *4—5 Disz tér, 13th century*

In the doorway of almost every house in Buda there were more or less decorated niches.
Nothing certain is known about their use: they may have been used by the visitors or
the servants having a rest here, or may have been in connection with the right of the
burghers to retail wine. The decoration of the niches must have been important for
every self—respecting householder. It is interesting that though building niches was
quite common in several Hungarian and foreign towns, it is only the characteristic of
Buda that there were niches in almost every house.

TIN TANKARD *from the well of the house at 10 Disz tér, c. 1350—1375.*
Almost every house in Buda had a cellar and a well hollowed in the rock. A large number of   interesting and valuable objects are found in them when they are dug out.

THE TOMB OF JOHN, A PAINTER OF THE KING (+ 1370).
A tomb with the coat of arms of one of the earliest guilds found at the Church of Our Lady

THE BUILDING COMPLEX OF THE ROYAL PALACE ≫→

A view from the Pest bank of the Danube in Hartman Schedel's World Chronicle (Nuremberg, 1493); and the plan of the excavated fragments (after Gerevich, 1966).
Most parts of the building complex of the royal palace were devastated in the ravages of the wars during the 150—year Turkish rule. In 1578 the lightning of a violent thunderstorm lit the gunpowder stored in the cellars of the first courtyard of the palace on the northern side, so all the buildings in the vicinity were ruined. The siege resulting in the reoccupation of the town in 1686 was especially destructive, as the still existing buildings were systematically destroyed from the direction of Gellérthegy by the artillery. The burnt walls were decaying for thirty years; then in 1715 they were pulled down, and the debris was put behind the newly—built ramparts. The lower levels of the palace filled with debris remained untouched, and thus it was possible to uncover them after the destruction of the 1944—1945 siege. Today by the help of the excavations and the contemporary written sources it is more or less possible to recontruct the building complex.

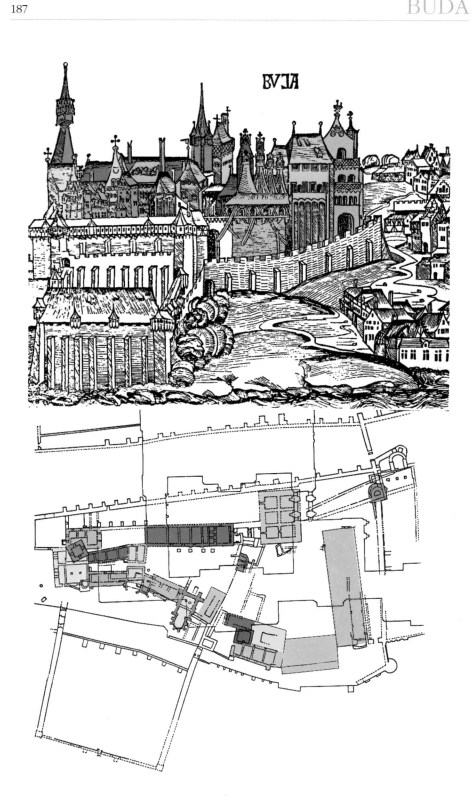

The main entrance of the palace opened to the town, from here two streets led to the spacious square outside the palace, in the middle of which King Matthias erected the bronze statue of Heracles. The square was separated from the castle with a wide moat hollowed in the rock, with a bridge across it. Behind the moat erected King Sigismund's enormous palace including a huge hall with wooden barrel vaulting on the upper level and under it another, two—aisled vaulted one. These halls were built first of all for receptions, wedding feasts and banquets. From the first courtyard of the palace a very wide staircase ornamented with statues led to the halls. On the Danube side of the first court the palace of King Matthias was situated, its door and window frames and stairs were made of marble, its bronze gate was decorated with reliefs depicting the deeds of Heracles; the whole palace, however, was not completed. On the opposite side of the yard there was a very wide square keep which was not built in its full height. The tower divided into six rooms was started by King Sigismund; but as it was not finished, it was called 'Csonkatorony' (incomplete tower), and its cellars were used as prisons. From this court the road led across a dry moat and through a gatehouse to the second court. On the two sides of the gate King Matthias stood bronze statues of unclothed, armed young men. This inner court was originally built in the time of King Luis, Queen Mary and King Sigismund; but King Matthias had it considerably rebuilt. The court was surrounded with a two—storey Renaissance loggia, the wooden ceiling of the upper level was decorated with the carved signs of the Zodiac. On the Danube side was the two—storey building of the ornamented royal chapel. The lower chapel kept its original form built by King Luis the Great. King Matthias had the upper chapel net—vaulted and its roof covered with coloured glazed tiles. He had the famous Corvina library built beside the chapel, it consisted of two tall halls with net vaulting and large windows, its walls were decorated with the horoscopes of King Wladislas II and Matthias. In the northern and western palace wings of the loggia court, several large halls were built, among them the throne room as well, which served as scenes of the administrative and political life the kingdom. In the middle of the courtyard a marble fountain was standing ornamented with bronze figures and the statue of Pallas Athene. The water was pressed up to the well from the Danube with the help of a hydraulic drive. There was one more gate opening from this court, leading into the most closed southern part of the palace. Here the residential buildings of the royal family and Stephen Tower formed a small courtyard. This was the oldest part of the palace, originaly constructed for Prince Stephen of the House of Anjou, and was rebuilt and enlarged several times. Beside the residential buildings the treasure and archives were kept here in the royal Treasury built to the Stephen Tower.

THE RECONSTRUCTED REMAINS OF THE STEPHEN TOWER

The southern part of Várhegy ends with a protruding rock lending itself to fortification; however, the earliest fortress, the castle of the Angevin Prince Stephen, called Stephen Tower can only be dated at the end of the 1340s, which can be regarded as the beginning of the royal palace. The few, disconnected fragments of walls found under the walls of Stephen Tower have nothing to do with the palace buildings, they must be the remains of an earlier, simple house. The Prince became the governor of the country at the age of 15, during the first campaign of King Luis to Naples in 1347; he was entitled to control Croatia, Slavonia and Dalmatia from 1350, but he died in 1354. (At the same time King Luis also had his seat in Buda between 1347 and 1355.) The castle of the Prince consisted of a square donjon and beside it buildings surrounding a courtyard; but the whole group of buildings occupied only the territory of an average site in Buda. It can be characterized by the traditional building style used in the 13th century: the palace wings stood at the edges of the rocky plateau on the eastern and western sides; in the south the rock and a big rectangular tower were used to close the yard and to fortify the whole castle. On the northern side its walls joined to the 13th century ramparts, i.e. enlarged and fortified them; so Stephen's Castle became the core of the huge building complex which developed in an area ideal for a town castle, in the later centuries of the Middle Ages.

THE ROYAL PALACE IN BUDA *in the 1390s*

While the Kammerhof, the old royal house, stood in the centre, surrounded by the houses of nobilities living in the town, Stephen's Castle joined the walls of the fortification in the narrow, much less important part of the town, far from the centre. That explains why King Luis I started enormous contruction work right in the foreground of Stephen's Castle from the second part of the 1370s, and why he gave away the Kammerhof in 1381, which he and his mother had enlarged in the 1340s.

The construction work started by King Luis, which was continued by Queen Mary and King Sigismund in the 1380s, was done according to large—scale plans and changed requirements. In front of the small Stephen's Castle a new, much wider courtyard was formed; this was only possible so that the facades of the palace wings were built not at the edge of the rocky plateau as before, but on the slope, in front of the spur of rock.

Both the eastern and the western wings follow the shape of the rocky plateau, thus creating a court, irregular in shape, widening from the south towards the north, almost forming a trapezeum. On the western side a rectangular building with a rather long facade was erected; on the eastern side, looking onto the Danube, the new royal chapel was built, with a palace wing beside it. Both new wings joined the buildings of Stephen's Castle. In the north a deep and wide rocky ditch separated the court from the town.

As the palaces and the new royal chapel were now on the slope, they had to be protected by building new ramparts. The palaces to the south of the ditch were surrounded by ramparts constructed homogeneously, with wooden machicolation placed on supports of the parapet. The south—western section of the ramparts has remained up to the level of the supports. On the eastern side the ramparts stretched southwards from the tower built at the end of the ditch, which was closed by the Csonkatorony on the west side. They ran in the direction of the outer facade of the Csonkatorony, which means that this huge keep was taken into considertion when the ramparts were planned. Other important parts of the ramparts were the curtain walls stretching as far as the Danube and enclosing the hillside, and at the same time defending the water supply and the harbour of the palace.

SHAPED BRICK WITH FLOWER MOTIF, *the last quarter of the 14th century.*
The large number of shaped bricks with different forms and motifs, found during the excavations shows that several palaces were built of this special kind of building block during the construction of the royal palace at the end of the 14th century. These bricks

used to decorate windows, gates, window sills were shaped and carved like stones, when still wet, before baking. Special expertise was needed to make them, as it was necessary to be skilled in stone carving as well making and baking bricks. Shaped bricks like the ones used in Buda have not been found in Hungary; but similar bricks can be seen on several churches, private and civic buildings in the north of Italy. The builders using shaped bricks to ornament the palaces in Buda must have arrived from there as well, they must have been invited by the king, and after finishing their work they returned to Italy. The use of motifs unusual in Hungary, continuing the antique traditions can also be explained by the Italian origin.

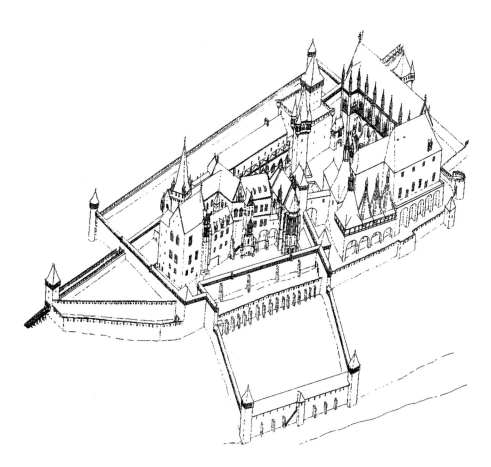

THE ROYAL PALACE *in the 1420s*

After an interval of about twenty years, in the 1410s King Sigismund began the large—scale enlargement of the palace. He moved the royal court from Visegrád to Buda already in 1408. By this time he managed to confirm his situation as a Hungarian king;

by the help of the Garai — Cillei League he conquered the rioters supporting Ladislas of Naples, the pretender to the throne in 1403; and then he had strong control over the coutry till the end of his life.

His power considerably grew when he was chosen German king in 1411. His firm position and increasing importance in international politics created the demand to enlarge the royal seat.

In this period of the construction another court surrounded by palaces was formed over the ditch closing the palace area earlier, after the civic houses were pulled down. The new court was separated from the town by a second ditch. The most important building of the court was a palace with huge halls, crossing the plateau behind the ditch. So far only some parts have been found; so it is only known from sources that the enormous building was about 70 m long and 25 m wide. The uppermost part housed one vast hall with wooden barrel vaulting, on the longer side its huge windows with transoms looked onto the town and the castle. Under this hall was a vaulted hall of similar size, but this was divided into two naves. The side of the court towards the Danube was also built in; but it has not been uncovered yet.

King Sigismund had Stephen's Castle rebuilt as well. To the eastern and western sides of the Stephen Tower very tall, four—storey buildings with small ground plans were attached. The building on the western side was joined to the tower, this housed the Treasury. The lower level and the remains of the staircase leading to the tower have been dug up. On the eastern side the residential part of the palace was extended with a new building. Its lower level covered with barrel vaulting has remained; and from the fragments it was possible to reconstruct the vaulted hall above it, which was divided by two pillars. On the uppermost level there was a bay window which has also been reconstructed from the stone carvings. Between the palace and the tower a spacious staircase was erected, which led directly into the garden.

The construction work can be dated from the fact that in about 1410 a new church for the chapter of the royal chapel was built outside the palace; in 1416 a master coming from Nuremberg, constructing the water conduit was mentioned; in 1418 the King sent stone carvers from Ulm and Ausburg to the construction work. According to his chronicle writer, Eberhard Windecke, the King returned from his long journeys in Europe into a new, expensive building in 1419.

The construction work in the 1410s ranked the Buda royal palace as one of the grandest royal residences of Eurpe.

KINGHTS AND HIS PAGE HOLDING HIS HELMET, *Gothic torsos, the 1420s*

In 1974 more than seventy torsos which can be adjusted and several thousand smalles or larger fragments of statues were found in the filled—up cellar of a burgher houses near the royal palace. This find gives a lot of information about the art of the royal court in Sigismund's time. The statues representing both religious and secular subjects are high standard works of art of the age. It has been proved that most of them were made in the same stone carving workshop, and have never been finished and erected. It is not known why they were used to fill up the cellar. The place of the find is situated halfway between the royal palace and the provostry of St. Sigismund; so it is difficult to decide where they were meant to stand, as when they were carved there was construction work going on both sites. In most of the cases they cannot be identified, as there are no coats of arms or other characteristic features. Their style suggests that first—class masters from different regions of Europe made them, first of all from two important areas. One group of masters represents the style of the French royal court, which was formed in the second half of the 14th century, and came to us through Burgundy and Brabant; the other shows close relationship with the works of art made in Grosslobming in Lower

Austria and Styria. These masters who had different qualifications and styles worked together in Buda, and created the statues of very high artistic value. The two torsos in the
picture are a typical pair among the statues with secular topics: a page rises the knight's
helmet, on which a panache, one part of the coat of arms, identifying the knight was
carved, but unfortunately it is missing.

FRAGMENT OF RENAISSANCE FRIEZE WITH DOLPHIN *from royal palace, red
marble, 1480s.*

After his second marriage to Beatrix of Aragon in 1476, King Matthias supported the
artists more and more generously. Through his wife's contacts, the King's interest was
arisen in the Italian Renaissance works of art with the mixture of their novelty and antiq-
uity. He went to great expenses to employ masters; and though he only sometimes managed to invite leading atrists, he gladly bought their works in Italy. He intended to re-
decorate his royal residence in the new style. However, the different styles were mixed,
as the elements of the new style were often used only as ornamentation in the well—
known late Gothic structures.

The construction work during the reign of King Matthias completely reformed the second court. The eastern wing was entirely pulled down to give room to the new building
of the library, with tall windows and covered with net vaulting. The neighbouring
chapel received net vaulting as well. Only the foundation walls of the building remained, but the debris were found at their foot. They are supposed to have been the
first, mostly still late Gothic construction work of the King; as written sources say on

one of the gates of the eastern wing the year of 1479 was to be read. The southern and western wings were not pullled down, but here all the window and door frames, cornices and fire places were replaced with Renaissance carvings. In front of the eastern, southern and western wings a two—level loggia was erected, which was completely destroyed. A lot of fragments of the balusters and pillars from the loggia have been found; the variety of their size and form proves that there must have been other loggias as well in other courts, too. On some red marble balustrades the coat of arms of Wladislas was already carved, as the buildings were not accomplished yet when Matthias died, and his successor finished them. Written sources mention that on one of the gates of the new building the year of 1502 and the name of Wladislas II were to be read. The building work in the first court was unfinished as well. Here the excavations uncovered the barrel vaulted cellars of a building covered with strange, pitched roofs seen in contemporary pictures. The palace with rich Renaissance ornamentation, often mentioned in sources, was situated to the north of this building; but its walls have not been uncoverd yet.

DETAIL OF MAJOLICA FLOORING, *the 1480s.*
King Matthias was very receptive to novelties, which was reflected in his patronage of the arts. In the last quarter of the 15th century the production of a new type of earthenware glazed with a new technique, called majolica started in Faenza. The King ordered for his palace ornamented floor tiles, vessels and tableware manufactured in Buda by masters coming from Faenza. The spoiled copies prove that they were really made here. Two types of floors were made: one consisted of big octogonal and small square tiles decorated mainly with coats of arms, the other of hexagonal and triangular tiles decorated with emblems and landscapes with wild animals.The works of the new style appeared first of all in the decoration. Written sources mention several bronze statues and candelabra ordered by the King; most of them, however, were taken away by Sultan Suleiman II in 1526. Today only the candlesticks probably from the chapel can be seen on the two sides of the Mihrab of Aya Sofia in Istanbul. The statue of Heracles on a marble pillar was an outstanding piece of art. As King Matthias was often compared to

Heracles by his contemporaries, it may have been a monument to the King depicted as a mythological figure; this was unique of its kind even in Italy. Even its placement in the middle of the square outside the palace was a novelty. The statues on the marble pillars on the two sides of the entrance to the second court, depicting unclothed young men imitated antique trophies, with allegories of victory on the sides of the pillars.

DETAIL OF THE PALACE GARDEN AND A FOUNTAIN WITH THE COATS OF ARMS OF KING MATTHIAS AND QUEEN BEATRIX, *the 1480s*

Almost every contemporary writer mentions the palace gardens, which were completely destroyed. On the southern part of the royal garden King Matthias had a hanging garden created beside the residential buildings and the Treasury. The garden was situated in the height of the rocky plateau, surrounded with palaces on three sides, and enclosed with an arcaded wall towards the slope. Under the hanging garden a cistern was dug, possibly the water of the Pallas well was led here. The lead pipes of the canal that ran from here to the gardens outside the ramparts as well as its bronze tap were uncovered. At the foot of the residential buildings behind the ramparts there were several enclosed gardens; in the southern courtyard another cistern has been opened up. The really big royal garden was beside the palace, outside the ramparts, stretching as far as the brook St. Paul (today Ördögárok). It was naturally enclosed with walls, all the more so as according to the descriptions game was also kept here. The pride of the garden must have been the still unknown palace, 'villa marmorea' built by King Matthias.

STOVE TILE *depicting King Matthias.*
Besides the fireplaces, the halls of the royal palace and the houses of the rich were heated with stoves made of coloured glazed tiles. The specially ornamented stoves made
for the king were masterpieces of the contemporary potters; and as they were quite soon
burnt and worn out, they were often replaced. This is the reason why in most cases
special topics, descriptions, coats of arms of certain periods can be seen on the stove
tiles.

THE SOUTHERN BIG ROUND BASTION OF THE BUDA CASTLE, *the 1530s.*
After the battle of Mohács, in the struggle between Ferdinand Hapsburg and John of
Szapolya, Buda was in the possession of King John from 1529 to his death. As he confirmed his position, the sovereign, who was threatened by the troops supporting the
Hapsburgs, strarted to fortify the town at the beginning of the 1530s. The southern fortification protecting the royal palace from the direction of Gellérthegy was built at this
time, which is the part of the King's fortifying work that remained the least damaged. A
round bastion was erected to replace the outdated gate from King Sigismund's period;
with its batteries it ensured the defence of the gentle slopes towards Gellérthegy and the
bank of the Danube. A covered casemate passage was joined to it, which led down to
the river. The bastion was already a symbol of a new period in which Buda lost its role
as the capital and   its peaceful life, and became a border fortification of key importance
in the Turkish times.

MATTHIAS' WEDDING

Matthias Hunyadi met his fiancée, Beatrix, the daughter of Ferinand of Aragon, the King of Naples, in Székesfehérvár on 10 December 1476. The Princess arrived from Naples with a magnificent retinue; and the celebratiation can also be called lavish and splendid. Peter Eschenloer, the notary of Boroszló, witnessed the events, and wrote about them with great enthusiasm: the coaches upholstered with velvet were driven by houses of the same colour; the ground was covered with thirteen rolls of blue broadcloth, which was torn into pieces at the end of the celebration as everybody wanted to take home something to commemorate the great day. The would—be wife gifted the King with a wreath with a diamond ring on it; they had actually contracted their marriage by proxy in Naples, as was the custom. After the reception, the Queen was crowned, which was conducted by the bishop of Veszprém. Eschenloer wrote about this as well. We also have the information from him that during the ceremony the King was wearing the regalia, so the Holy Crown as well; and that the Queen took an oath, though we do not know its text. The crown which was put on the head of Beatrix was made of gold and was ornamented with diamonds, rubies and sapphires; the Holy Crown was only held above the Queen's shoulder during the act of anointment.

The most sumptuous celebrations, however, were in Buda. It is worth quoting the words of a Bavarian traveller, Hans Seybolt about even the entry: 'It looked like snow when the King rode into the town with his bride. The retinue with the sacrements also returned to the town. After the sacrements about two thousand five hundred knights rode dressed in splendid suits of armour decorated with plumes. They were followed by the representatives of the guilds. Then sixty—seven drummers and trumpeters were riding dressed in red damask pelisses; they were followed by twenty—five saddle—horses wonderfully armoured and bridled with riders wearing the King's colours .... Then the King's eleven young horsemen were riding tall horses with pearl flowers on the forehead and pearls on the saddlery of the horses, and the coats of arms of Hungary and Bohemia on the shields and breastplates of the knights, all embroidered with pearls. These young men were wearing German clothes, just like the King, who was riding beside the Queen; his suit was also covered with pearls. His coat was in German style, on his head was a hat decorated with a crown of pearls and precious stones, on his side a gold sword; with saddlery with pearls, gold and precious stones on his horse and a crown of precious stones on the forehead of his horse.'

On the following days the celebrations were continued in the Buda palace, mostly in the palace wing built by Sigismund, respectively in its foreground. On 17 December the King gave a grand dinner party about which and the days to follow not only Seybolt but the legates of the Saxon and Pflaz princes report as well.

That is why we have information about the plan of the palace and that beside the big dining hall, possibly on the first floor, there was a smaller room at the convenience of the guests, which was heated, called 'hypocaustum', which refers to the way of heating. The legate from Pfalz highly praised the big hall:

'The dining hall was ornamented with sumptuous red curtains inter-twined with gold and pearl, rarity worthy of a king. '

Everything must have been overshadowed by the feast after the royal wedding on 22 December in the same hall, the size of which was impressive: it was 70 m long, 18—20 m wide, two—aisled with nine pillars in the middle, and eight—level buffets around the pillars.

'The platters, the goblets of the King and Queen and the wines of magnates were placed here to be at the service of the royal table. On the other seven shelves there were gold and silver wine—jugs, cups and ladles, all delicate goldsmith work. On the lowerest lever two silver unicorns were standing with real horns' — writes one of the legates about the buffet in front of the King's table; then continues the description of the hall as follows:

'In front of the table on the floor a marvellously formed, unique fountain was standing of three hundred pounds of silver, it was so tall that its opening was hardly accessible even for an adult man. Beside the fountain five silver wickerwork baskets were placed.

Silver barrels with taps were hanging above, the wine was drawn from them for the royal couple and the guests. ... There were nine hundred and eighy—three dishes on the buffets not counting the cups and jugs in use. ... In the front there was a round table, behind it a golden curtain was hanging in the whole length of the wall. Above the table on the ceiling there were three big tapestries intertwined with gold. On one of them were the coats of arms of the Queen, in two shields with two crowns, on the other two those of the King were to be seen.'

Seybolt gives detailed description of the dishes served at the feast :

'The first course was dessert. In the second living birds sang, the third course was black game, the fourth minced meat in white and brown slices, the fifth formed a golden box tree with angels and squirrels, in the sixth there were guinea fowl and capons standing on yellow apples. The seventh course imitated an enclosed garden. On the fence there were birds sitting, in the middle of the garden a golden myrtle was standing with brown and green pears and cakes as big as a coconut. Everything was made of burnt sugar. The eighth course was rice, the ninth game again, the tenth fricassee of chicken in some kind of yellow sauce and finally the eleventh was daughnuts.' We also have information about the seating and the guests invited, from the Pfalz legate. He says that at the royal table the following were sitting: the King and the Queen, to the right the son of the king of Naples, the archbishop, legates of princes and kings then guests from

Ferrara and Venice. Closest to the Queen Christopher, the Prince of Bavaria was sitting, beside him the palatine with Saxon nobilities, and then Luis and Otto, Bavarian princes with their advisers.'

Besides the table of the King, which — as described — was 22 steps long, there were several other tables in the hall, which were situated lengthwise. Among the guests sitting here was the King's mother Elizabeth Szilágyi and other ladies, the lower—ranking members of the Naples legation and Hungarian dignitaries and clergymen.

After the feast the tables were removed and the day was finished with a ball.

Naturally the usual tournament was also held. Seybolt writes about this as follows: 'Prince Christopher jousted Prince Hinco of Bohemia. Both fell out of their saddles. Two more knights had a fight. The tournament took one and a half hours. In the inner rooms clowns entertained' those who were not interested in the spectacular fight of the knights.

GIANFRANCO ROMANO: BEATRIX OF ARAGON AND MATTHIAS HUNYADI
Marble bas-relief, 1489
The bas-relief of the royal couple, made a year before the king's death depicts the Renessaince sovereign' and his wife in contemporary fashion.

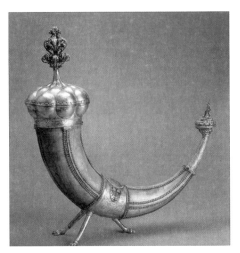

GLASS GOBLET, *considered to have belonged to Kind Matthias*
The goblet was given to the Batthyányi family by Luis II, and the museum received it from their collection. The inscription carved into its foot says once King Matthias drank out of it.

HORN GOBLET *from the 15th century royal court*
Goblets of bison horn richly ornamented with silver and gold were fashionable in Hungary in the 15th century. Such and similar goblets must have been used at the wedding feast of King Matthias.

MAJOLICA PLATE WITH THE COATS OF ARMS MATTHIAS AND BEATRIX
The Queen, who came from Naples, brought some new habits and customs into her husband's court. The fashion of majolica plates in Italian style started at this time, too.

THRONE TAPESTRY OF KING MATTHIAS: VELVET BROCADE WITH GOLDEN EMBROIDERY, *the 1480*

Though the throne tapestry was made later than those hanging in the Great Hall in Buda during the wedding feast, this suggests the pomp of that event.

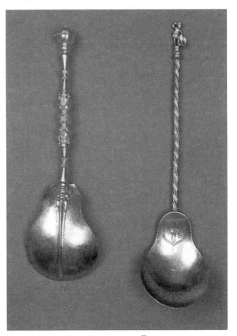

GOBLET FROM THE KÖLESD
TREASURES

This unique silver goblet may be similar
to the ones in the buffets in the Buda
royal palace, none of which have
remained; descriptions suggest that they
were used in large numbers.

SPOONS FROM THE KÖLESD
TREASURES

Silver cutlery. During most of the Middle
Ages only knives were used; spoons were
only used later, there is data about forks
only from the 15th century. In big feasts it
was still a general habit to eat with hands.
King Matthias was said to be very clever,
he never stained his clothes with sauces.

CHRONOLOGY

1241 April After the Mongol troops led by Batu Khan defeat the Hungarian royal army at Muhi (11 April) near the River Sajó, they occupy, ransack and burn Pest.

The beginning of 1242 The Mongols cross the frozen Danube, occupy and destroy Óbuda.

1244 24 November King Béla IV renews the letters—patent of the Buda settlers, 'hospes' (this is the basis of the privileges of Buda later).

1247 Hearing about another Mongol attack Béla IV begins to build the Buda castle to fortify the line of the Danube and protect the Pest 'hospes'.

The 1250s The first data about the Jews in Buda. (The oldest Jewish tomb in Buda is from 1278)

1254 The Dominican Order has the yearly general chapter in the new friary in Buda. The Franciscan and Augustinian friaries are also built about this time.

1254—1270 Béla IV's pious daughter, Margaret lives in the Dominican convent founded on the Island of Rabbits.

1255 25 July Béla IV bestows the market tax of the town of Buda and the advowson of St. Mary's Church (later the parish church of Our Lady) to be built in the castle on the Dominican convent on the Island of Rabbits.

c. 1255 A coin mint starts to work in Buda.

1255—1269 The three—aisled church of Our Lady, the parish church of the Germans is built. The Hungarians have only the small, one—aisled Mary Magdalen's Church in the castle and the church of St. Peter the Martyr in the suburb.

1269 Béla IV puts the newly—built church of Our Lady in Buda under the authority of the bishop of Veszprém.

1270 3 May Béla IV dies on the Island of Rabbits, his successor is his son, Stephen V.

1272 6 August Stephen V dies, his successor is Ladislas (Cuman) IV. Stephen V is buried on the Dominican convent on the Island of Rabbits, beside his sister, Margaret.

1279 September The Buda council meets led by Philip, papal legate.

1290 10 July Ladislas (Cuman) IV dies.

1301 14 January Andrew III, the last king of the House of Árpád dies in Buda and is buried in the Franciscan church.

1301 August Wenceslas, Czech heir to the throne arrives in Buda.

1302 September Charles Robert besieges Buda unsuccessfully, destroys the vineyards of the burghers. Cardinal Nicolas, papal legate interdicts Buda.

1304 August Wenceslas II returns to Bohemia with his son, takes the Buda rector, László, the son of Werner as a prisoner, appoints Peturmann, the son of Kunc as rector. On his behalf Lajos, a priest in Buda exempts the town from the interdict and excommunicates the pope and the bishops of the country.

1305 The Order establishes its 'studium generale' in the Buda Dominican friary. (It was the institution of the medieval Hungary, which granted the highest qualifications)

1307 1 June László, the son of Werner

flees, takes the town of Buda by ruse for Charles Robert. Peturmann flees, the heretic priests are handed over to the archbishop of Esztergom.

1309 15 June Tamás, the Archbishop of Esztergom crowns Charles Robert with a new crown in the church of Our Lady in Buda (Charles Robert's second coronation).

1311 25 June Máté Csák attacks Charles Robert with his troops in Buda and destroys the surroundings of the town.

1332 20 March A blaze destroys the town.

c. 1334 Bailiff Wulving, a Buda burgher founds a chapel in honour of the three Hungarian saint kings in the cemetery of the church of Our Lady (later known as St. Ladislas' chapel).

1342 16 July Charles Robert dies.

1342 17—18 July Charles Robert's body is taken to Buda from Visegrád and lay in state in the church of Our Lady.

1347 January—1355 September The royal court moves to Buda from Visegrád.

The end of the 1340s The 'Stephen's Castle' is built in the southern end of the town for Prince Stephen of the House of Anjou, the brother of King Luis the Great.

c. 1349 Queen Mother, Elizabeth builds St. Martin's Church in the Kammerhof.

The 1360s Luis the Great expels the Jews from the whole country.

1365 November Charles IV, Emperor of the Holy Roman Empire stays in Buda to propose Princess Elizabeth for his son, Wenceslas.

1366 spring—summer John (Palailogos), Byzantine emperor negotiates with Luis the Great in Buda.

1368 25 February Casimir III, Polish king enters into a commercial contract with Luis the Great.

c. 1371 Luis the Great builds a chapel in honour of St. George in the market place of the town and appoints a rector independent of the parsons.

1372 Luis the Great and his mother, Queen Elizabeth found the Carmelite friary called 'Mother of Mercy' in the suburb, Taschental.

The end of the 1370s — the beginning of the 1380s Luis the Great begins to enlarge the 'Stephen's Castle', the building is continued by his daughter, Queen Mary and King Sigismund.

1381 autumn Luis the Great bestows the old royal mansion, the Kammerhof on the Pauline friary so that they can keep the relic of Hermit St. Paul there in case of danger.

1382 10 September Luis the Great dies.

1382 After the death of Luis the Great the court is again in Buda.

1384 The tower of the church of Our Lady collapses during a Mass.

1386 7 February Balázs Forgách, treasurer inflicts a mortal wound on Charles (Small) II in the royal palace. The houses of the Italian merchants are broken into and robbed.

1388 March King Sigismund has István Hédervári Kont and thirty—two others beheaded, because they revolt againt him, in the market place of the town in St. George Square (today Disz tér). They are buried in Corpus Christi Chapel.

The beginning of the 1400s The small Mary Madgalen's

Church is pulled down and a three—aisled church is built. The Dominican and Franciscan friaries are also considerably enlarged and rebuilt.

1408   King Sigismund moves the royal household and offices to Buda.

c. 1410   Sigismund founds a new church in honour of St. Mary and St. Sigismund for the royal chapel outside the royal palace in the old Zsidó utca (Jewish Street).

The 1410s   Sigismund considerably enlarges the royal palace, so several houses of the burghers are pulled down. The Buda royal residence is equal to the biggest royal palaces in Europe with its size and decoration.
The church of Our Lady is rebuilt, new side chancels are constructed and the nave is reshaped into a hall.

1424 June—July Sigismund receives John (Palaiologos) VIII, Byzantine emperor and Eric VII, the king of Denmark, Sweden and Norway, in his Buda palace.

1437 9 December Sigismund, the King of Hungary and the Emperor of the Holy Roman Empire dies in Znojmo, Moravia. His successor is his son—in—law, Albert Hapsburg, Austrian Prince.

1439 May   There are disturbances between the German and Hungarian inhabitants of Buda, the houses of foreign merchants are plundered. As a result the Hungarian burghers receive equal rights with the Germans.

1439 27 October Albert, who became ill in the campaign against the Turks, dies in   Neszmély.

After 1441   The alliance of seven free royal towns expropriates the Court

of Appeal, the court of justice of the Treasurer. The towns are directed, the jurisdiction is administered according to the Buda Law—book.

1444 The centre of the province of the Hungarian Observant Franciscans is the Buda friary.

1444 10 November The Hungarian army suffers a serious defeat from the Turks in the Varna battle, Wladislas I dies.

1457 14 March In Buda Ladislas V arrests the Hunyadi brothers, Ladislas and Matthias, responsible for the death of Ulric Cillei, and their supporters.

1457 16 March Ladislas Hunyadi is beheaded in the square outside the royal palace in the evening. His body is taken to Mary Magdalen's Church and is buried in the Chapel of Corpus Christi in the suburb. (Later he is taken to Gyulafehérvár) Matthias is kept in custody in the treasury.

1457 the beginning of June
Ladislas V goes to Vienna, later to Prague with the captive Matthias.
23 November Ladislas V dies in Prague.

1458 24 January After the prelates and lords agree about the succession to the crown, the gentry proclaims Matthias Hunyadi king on the frozen Danube.

1458 14 February King Matthias is seated on the throne in the church of Our Lady in Buda (The Holy Crown is in the possession of Emperor Frederick III).
Matthias appoints a court marshal to control the royal estates centrally.

1461   The Jews of Buda build a new two—aisled Gothic synagogue.

1461 May Matthias marries Catherine of

Podebrad, Czech Princess, in the church of Our Lady in Buda.

1464 February Catherine of Podebrad dies and is buried in the church of the chapter of St. Mary or St. Sigismund, situated in front of the palace.

The 1470s Andreas Hess, a typographer from Nuremberg, has a printing house in Buda. His most significant book is 'Chronica Hungarorum' also called the Buda Chronicle.

The southern tower of the church of Our Lady and a royal oratory are built on the southern side of the church.

The middle of the 1470s Matthias establishes a Jewish national prefecture led by the Mendel family of Buda.

1476 22 December Matthias marries Beatrix of Aragon, Princess of Naples, in the church of Our Lady in Buda.

The end of the 1470s — the beginning of the 1490s

Matthias has the Buda palace significantly rebuilt by builders from Florance and Dalmatia in al'antica Renaissance style. The construction is finished by Wladislas II.

1490 6 April King Matthias I dies in Vienna.

The 1490s Mary Magdalen's Church is lengthened and a new tower is added.

1503 February The Fugger Firm from Ausburg establishes a branch in Buda to deal with credits and to control the copper export of Hungary.

1506 26 July Wladislas II's wife, Ann of Candale dies. She is buried in the church of the chapter of St. Mary or St. Sigismund, situated in front of the palace.

1516 13 March Wladislas II, the King of Hungary and Bohemia dies in Buda. He is succeeded on the throne by his son, Luis II, the King of Hungary and Bohemia.

1526 29 August The Hungarian army suffers a crushing defeat from the Turkish troops led by Suleiman II in the Mohács battle. Luis II dies while fleeing.

1526 14—29 September Suleiman II occupies Buda deserted by the inhabitants. The town is plundered and then burnt except for the royal palace.

1529 8 September Suleiman II occupies the town defended by Tamás Nádasdy after a short siege as the German merceneries surrender.

1530 October—November Wilhelm Roggendorf unsuccessfully besieges Buda protected by King John.

The 1530s King John has Italian military engineers fortify Buda.

1540 21 July King John dies.

1541 29 August After Wilhelm Roggendorf unsuccessfully besieges Buda protected by Friar George and Bálint Török, the army of the Sultan destroys the besieging troops and occupies the town. The Hungarian guards are expelled; the infant John Sigismund and his supporters are sent to Transylvania. Buda is under Turkish rule for 150 years.

BIBLIOGRAPHY

GENERAL

Budapest Történetének Okleveles Emlékei (The history of Budapest in charters) vol. I. Ed. by Dezső Csánky and Albert Gárdonyi. Budapest 1936. vol. III. Ed. by Bernát L. Kumorovitz Budapest 1987.
Budapest Múemlékei (The monuments of Budapest) Ed. by Frigyes Pogány vol I. Budapest 1955. vol. II. Budapest 1962.
Huszár, Lajos: A budai pénzverés története a középkorban (The history of coin minting in the Middle Ages) Budapest 1958.
Ofner Stadtrecht. Hg. v. Károly Mollay. Budapest 1959.
Rózsa, György: Budapest régi látképei (1493—1800) (Old picture of Budapest) Budapest 1963.
Gerevich, László: The Art of Buda and Pest in the Middle Ages. Budapest 1971.
Budapest története (The history of Budapest) Ed. László Gerevich. vol. I—II. Budapest 1973.
Zolnay, László: Az elátkozott Buda — Buda aranykora. (The accursed Buda — the golden age of Buda) Budapest 1982.
Towns in the medieval Hungary. Ed. by László Gerevich. Budapest 1990.
Budapest im Mittelalter. Hg. v. Gerd Biegel. Brauschweig 1991.

THE ROYAL PALACE

Gerevich, László: A budai vár feltárása (The excavations in the Buda castle) Budapest 1966.
Balogh, Jolán: Művészet Mátyás király udvarában (Art in King Matthias' court) I—II. Budapest 1976.
Zolnay, László—Szakál, Ernő: A budavári gótikus szoborlelet (The Gothic statues found in Buda) Budapest 1976.
Zolnay, László: Az 1967—75. évi budavári

ásatásokról és az itt talált gótikus szoborcsoportról. (About the excavations in Buda in 1967—75 and the Gothic statues found here) Budapest régiségei XXIV/3—4. (1977) pp 5—152.
Zolnay, László—Marosi, Ernő: A budavári szoborlelet (The statues found in Buda) Budapest 1987.
Gerő, László: A helyreállított budai vár (The reconstructed Buda castle) Budapest 1980.

THE CHURCH OF OUR LADY (MATTHIAS' CHURCH)

Némethy, Lajos: Nagyboldogasszonyról nevezett budapestvári főtemplom története (The history of the church of Our Lady in Budapest) Esztergom 1876.
Csemegi, József: A budavári főtemplom középköri építéstörténete (The history of teh construction of the church in Buda) Budapest 1955.
Entz, Géza: A Mátyás-templom és a Halászbástya (Matthias' Church and the Fishermen's Bastion) Budapest 1987.

MARY MAGDALEN'S CHURCH

Bertalan, Vilmosné: Előzetes jelentés a Mária Magdolna-templom ásatásairól (A report about the excavations in the Mary Magdalen's Church) Budapest Rég. XXII (1971) pp 419—428.

DOMINICAN FRIARY

H. Gyürki, Katalin: Das mittelalterliche Dominikanerkloster in Buda. Fontes Archaeologici Hungariae. Budapest 1981.

SYNAGOGUES

Zolnay, László: Buda középkori zsidósága és zsinagógáik (The Jews in the medieval Buda and their synagogues) Budapest 1987.

THE OPENING HOURS OF THE MUSEUMS

Budapesti Történeti Múzeum (Budapest Historical Museum)
Vármúzeum (Castle Museum) Budavári Palota, Building E
Open: March to October: 10 am—6 pm
     November: 10 am—5 pm
     December to January: 10 am—4 pm
     February: 10 am—5 pm
     Closed on Tuesday

Medieval Synagogue
1014 Budapest I., Táncsics Mihály utca 26.
Open: May — October on weekdays:
10 am—2 pm
at the weekend: 10 am — 6 pm C
Closed on Monday

Gül Baba's Mausoleum
1023 Budapest II., Mecset utca 14.
Open: May—October 10 am—6 pm, closed on Monday

CONTENTS